Lyrics *of the* Sands

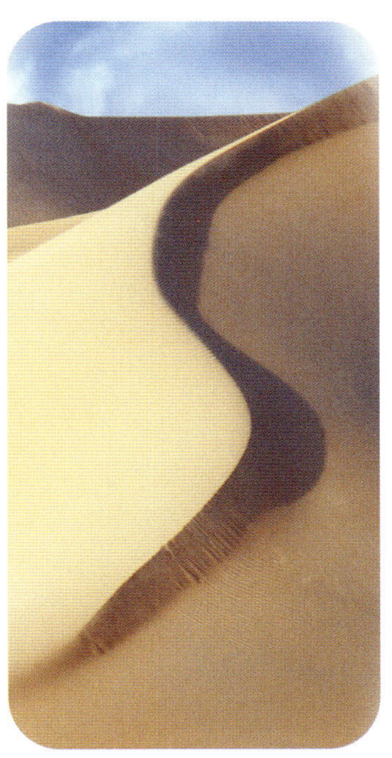

Gloria Kifayeh

LYRICS OF THE SANDS
published by
Stacey International
128 Kensington Church Street
London W8 4BH
Tel: 020 7221 7166 Fax: 020 7792 9288
E-mail: enquiries@stacey-international.co.uk
Website: www.stacey-international.co.uk

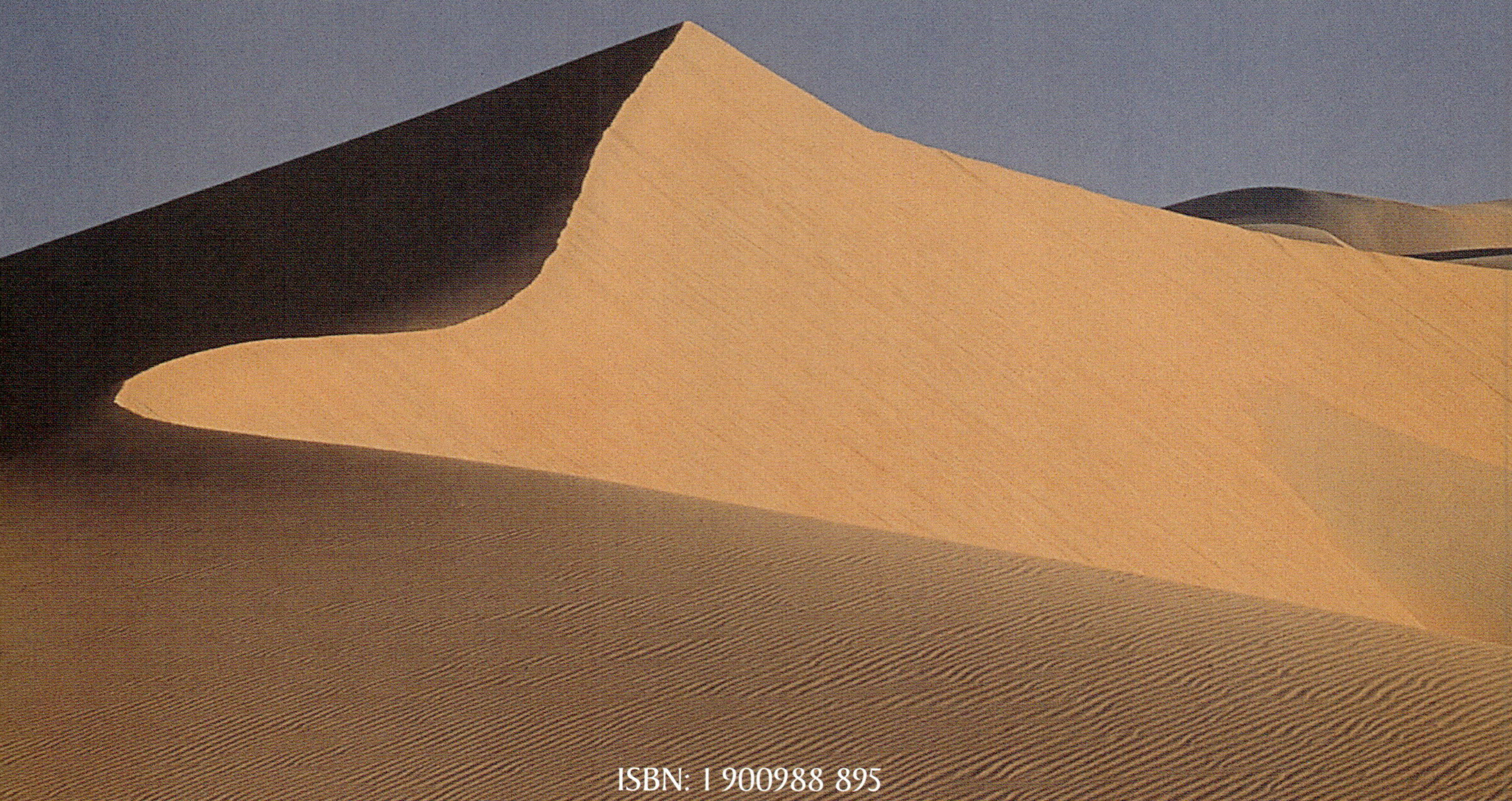

ISBN: 1 900988 895

CIP Data: A catalogue record for this book is available from the British Library

Design: Graham Edwards
Printing & Binding: SNP Leefung, China

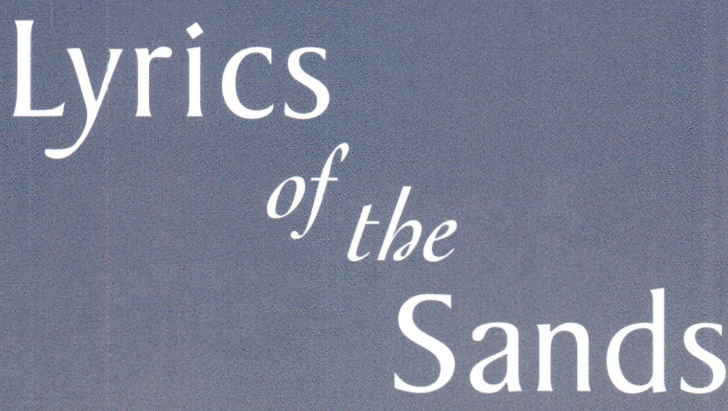

Lyrics
of the
Sands

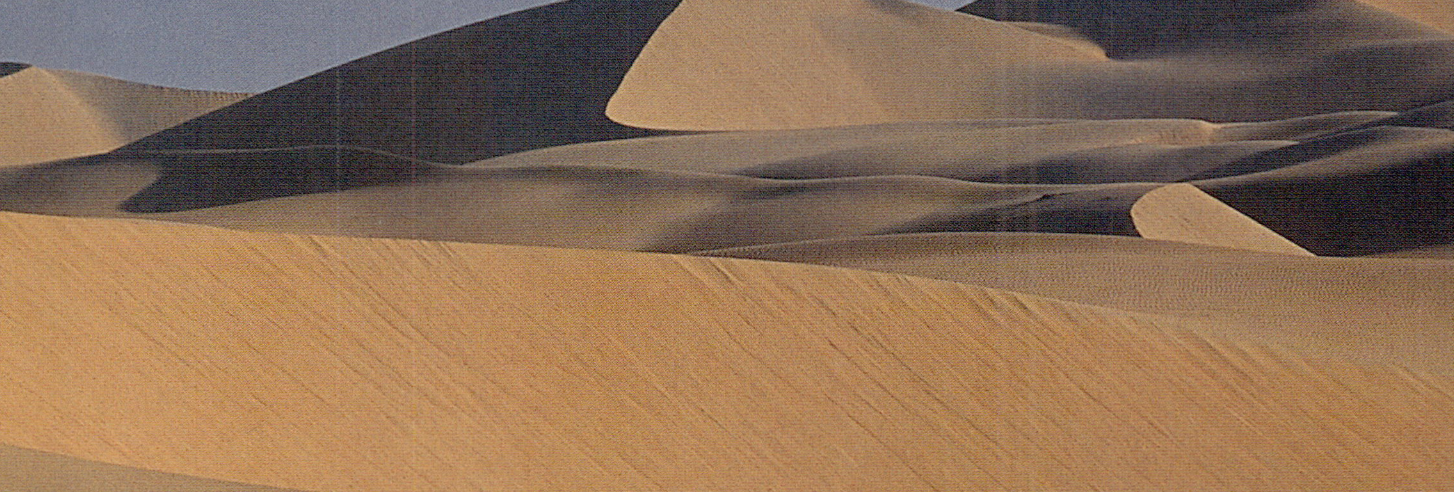

Gloria Kifayeh

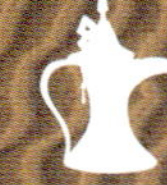

STACEY INTERNATIONAL
London

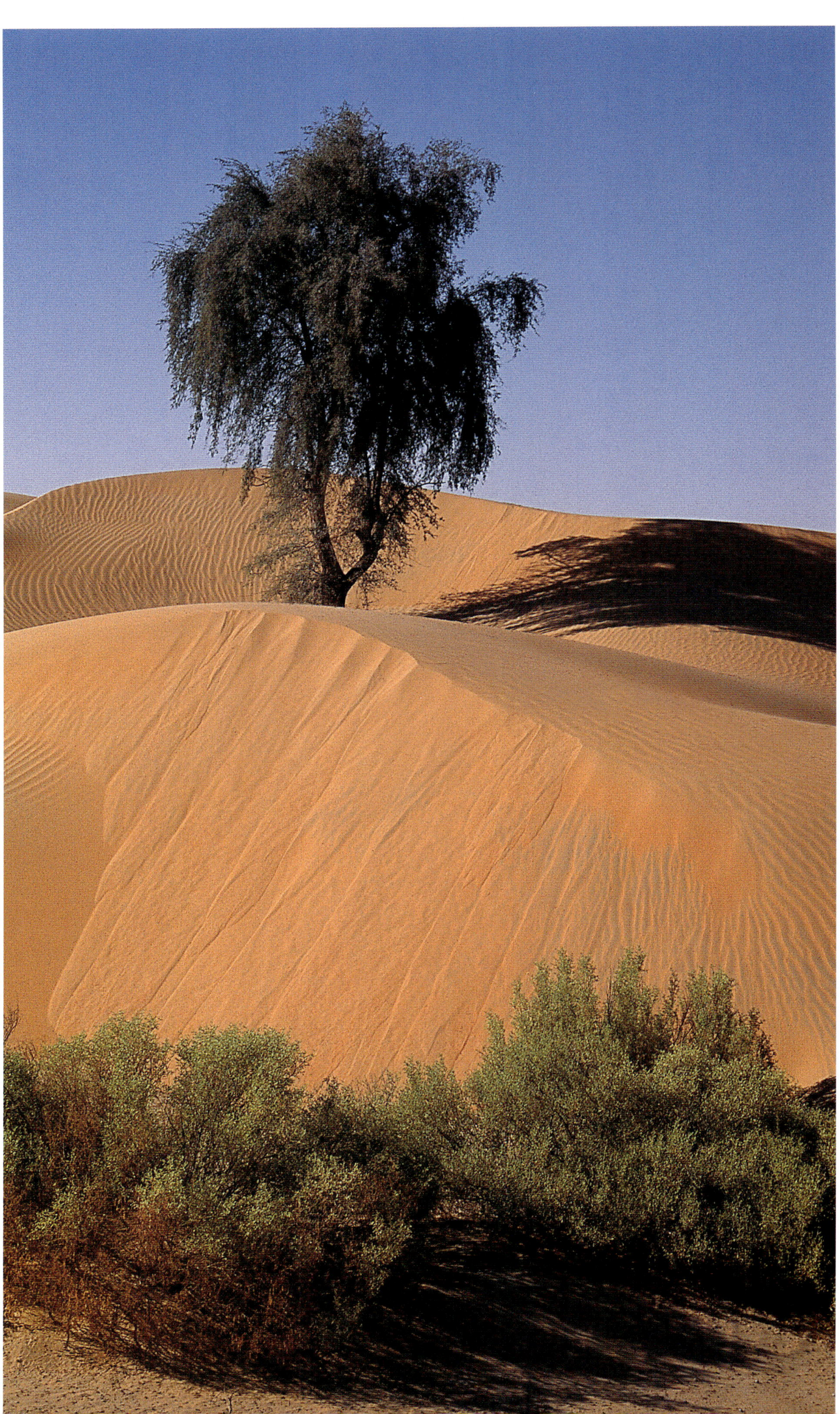

Foreword

The lens of the photographer captures remote beauty to reveal it on paper ~ or screen ~ to an audience that has perhaps never had the opportunity to experience it first hand. Before such technology, travellers conveyed that beauty to their audience by language, the written word, or song or recitation.

Lyrics of the Sands places the camera artistry of Gloria Kifayeh alongside excerpts from the very first recorded Arabian desert poetry ~ creative spirits united by a common theme but separated by fourteen centuries.

The photographs of Gloria Kifayeh ~ her work so widely acclaimed ~ speak for themselves. A brief word on the pre-Islamic (*jahiliyyah*) poetry may assist in interpreting the text. Spoken Arabic poetry had already evolved into a refined form by the time it was first captured in written script around the period of the birth of Islam in the early Seventh century CE. It thus 'arrived' intact, already perfectly formed, to provide the foundation for all future creative writing in Arabic.

The immeasurably ancient oral heritage of the Bedouin poets stemmed from the manner of Bedouin life. Disciplined by rhyme and metre, the medium flourished, expressing the hopes and fears of the wandering tribal community. The themes were honour, love, prowess in battle, and resilience in the face of the constant threats posed by the fierce sun and the rugged terrain, exiguous sustenance and the vulnerability of human existence.

The verses offered here serve only as a hint of the richness and glory of their poetic genre. Yet we hope that, coupled with the enchantment of the photography they will lead the reader to a deeper knowledge of *jahiliyyah* poetry.

Key titles for further reading might be A J Arberry's *Arabic Poetry: A Primer for Students* or Alan Jones' two volume *Early Arabic Poetry,* both of which present the original Arabic alongside a translation.

Max Scott
November 2004

أَمِنْ آلِ أَسْمَاء الطَّلَلُولُ الدَّوَارِسُ   يُخَطِّطُ فِيهَا الطَّيرُ قَفْرٌ بَسَابِسُ

المُرَقِّشُ الأَكْبَر

Did these barely visible traces of a campsite once belong to Asma's family?
Now birds trace their marks across them ~ there is no human here ~ a wilderness.

Al-Muraqqish al-Akbar

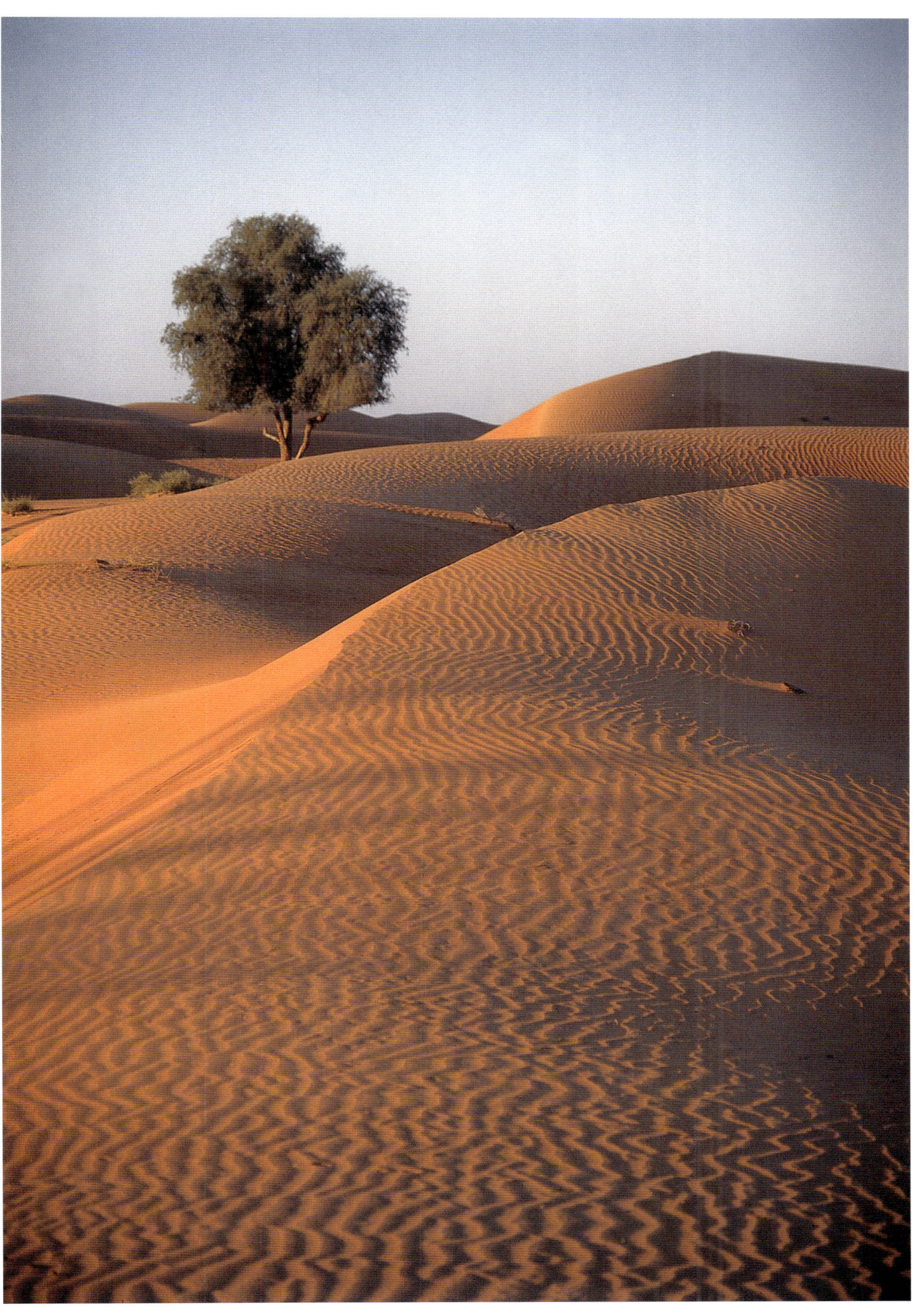

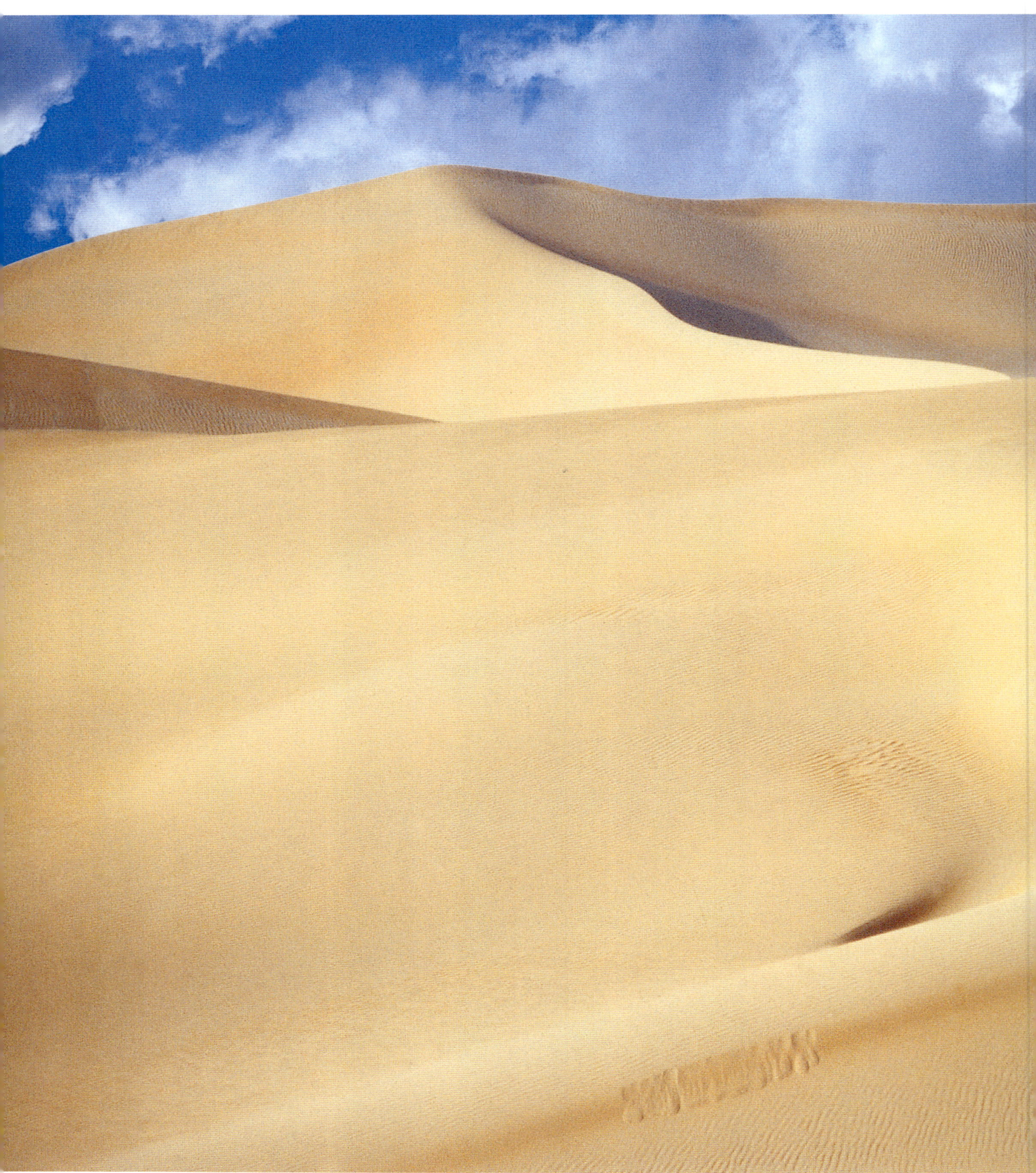

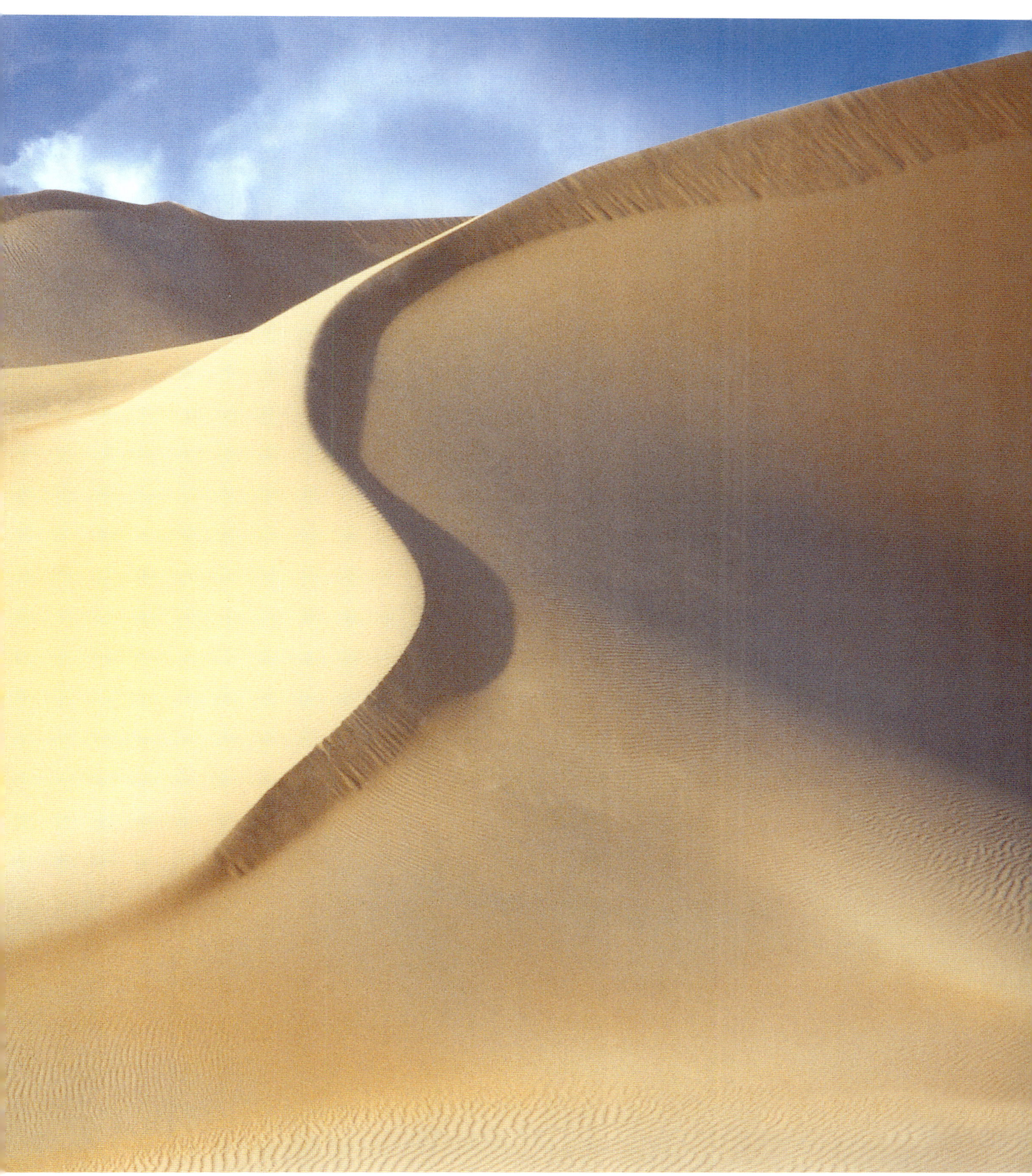

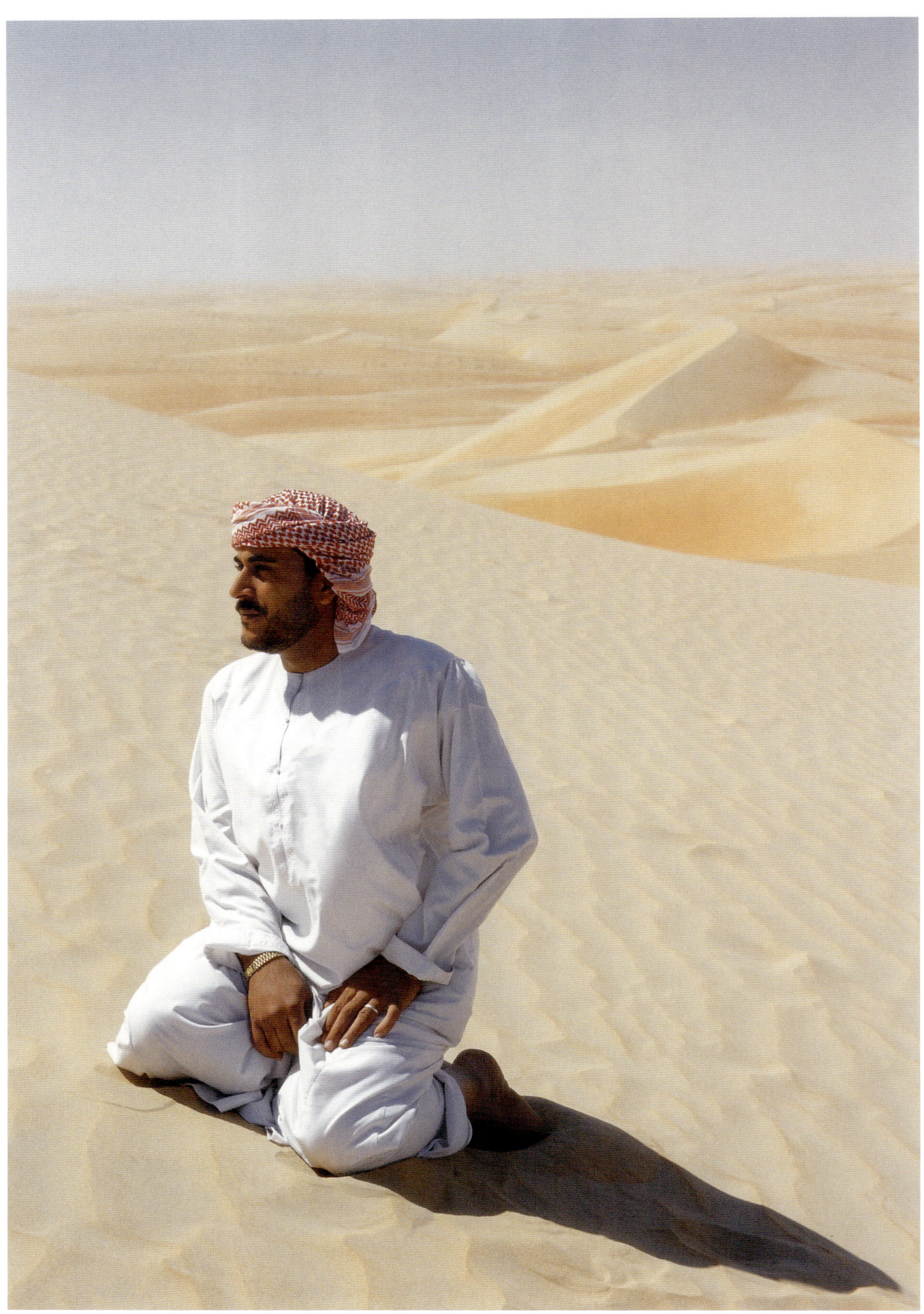

وَخَرْقٍ كَظَهْرِ التُرْسِ قَفْرٍ قَطَعْتُهُ   بِعَامِلَتَيْنِ ظَهْرُهُ لَيْسَ يُعْمَلُ

الشَّنْفَرىٰ الأَزْدِي

Many a wind-swept desert I have crossed, uninhabited and bare
like the back of a shield, its surface untrodden by any other human foot.

Al-Shanfara al-Azdi

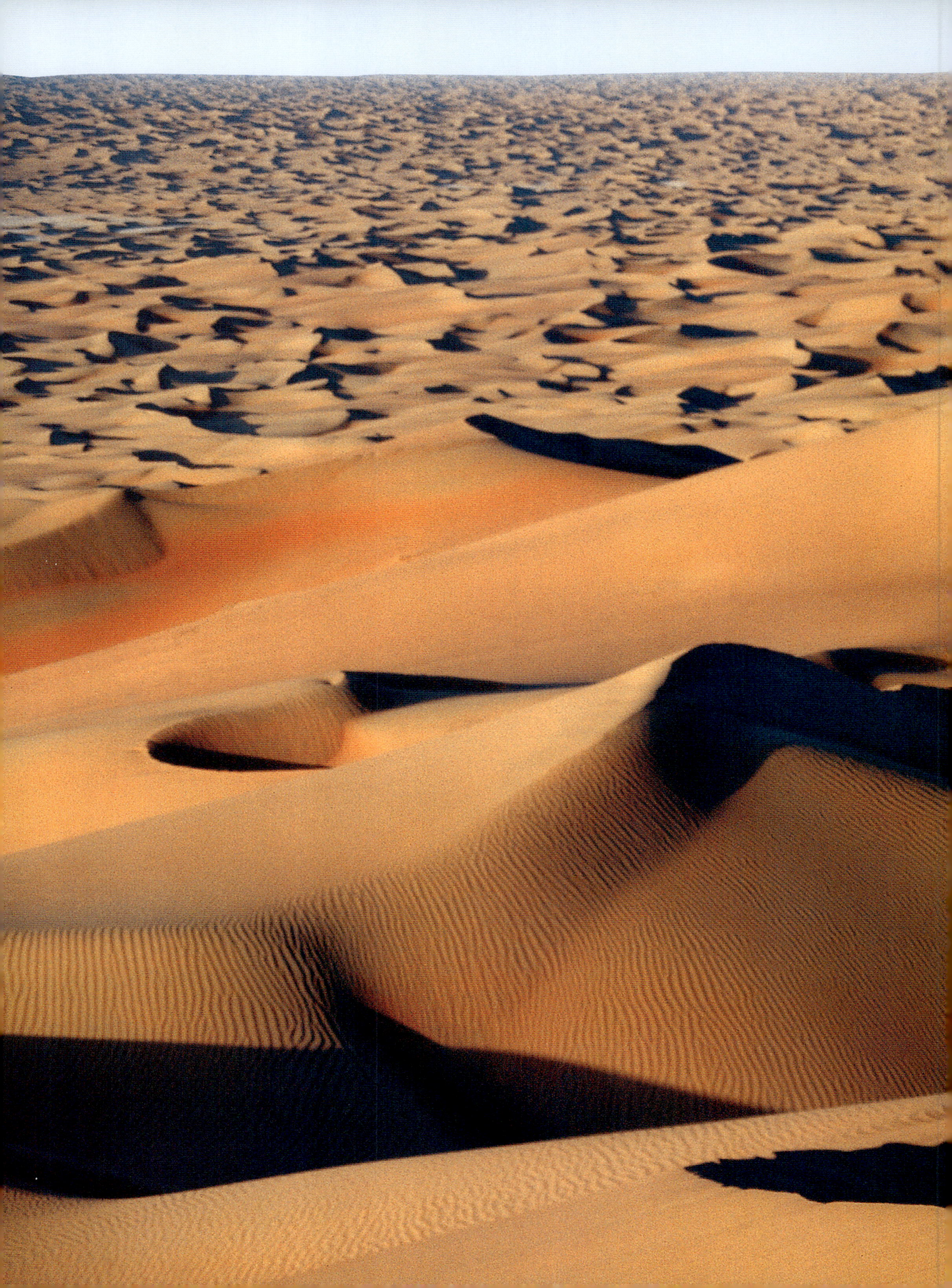

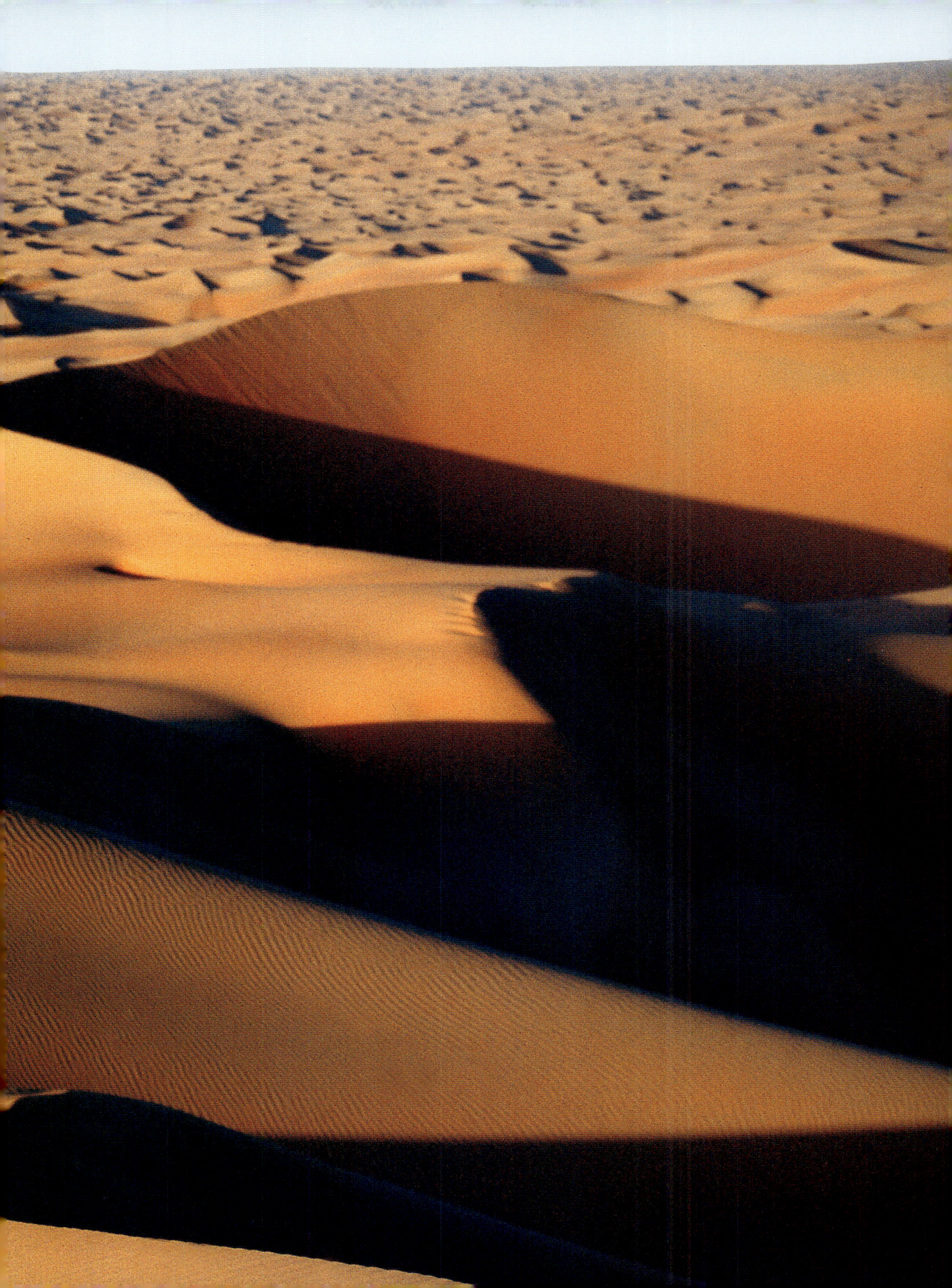

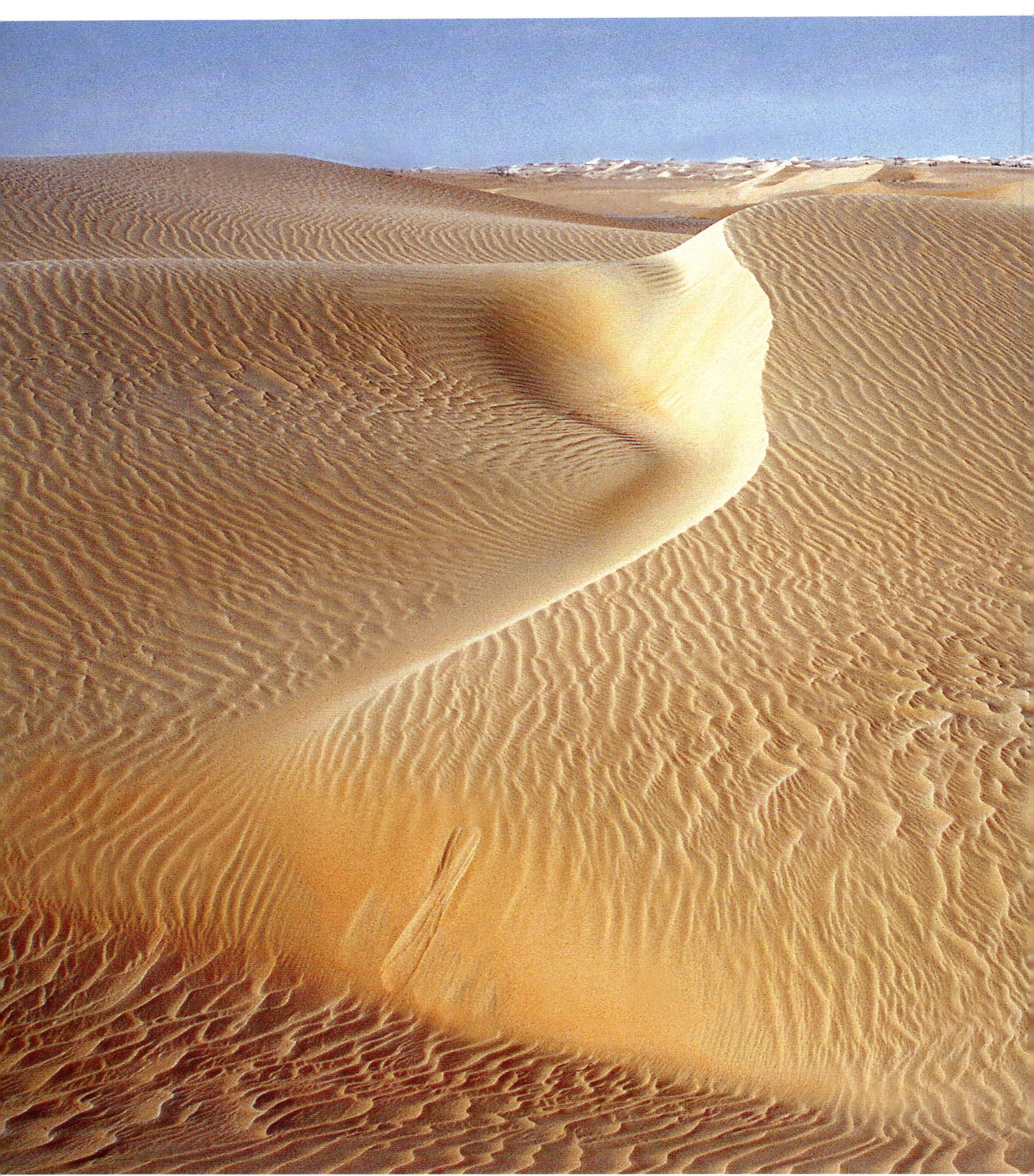

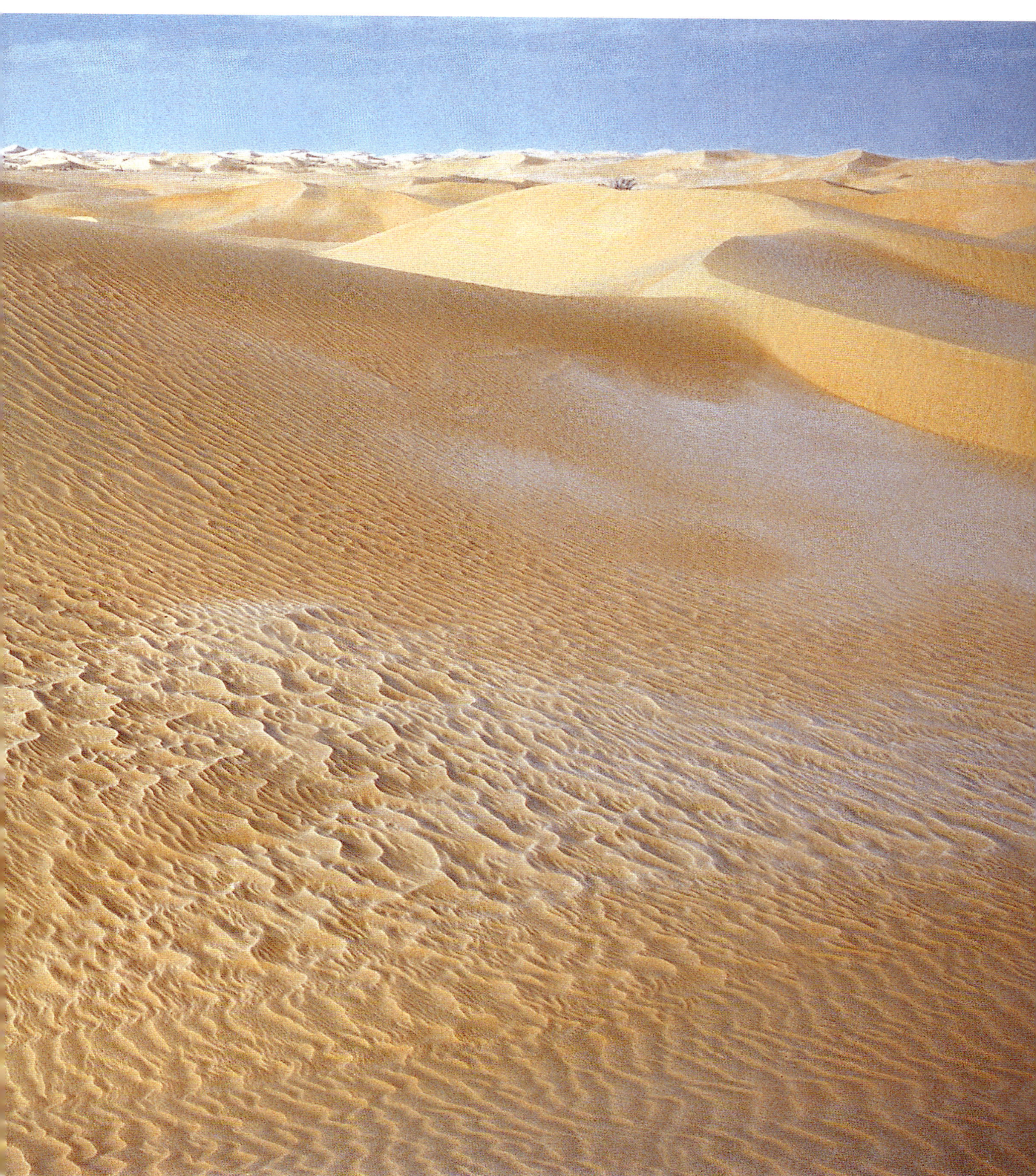

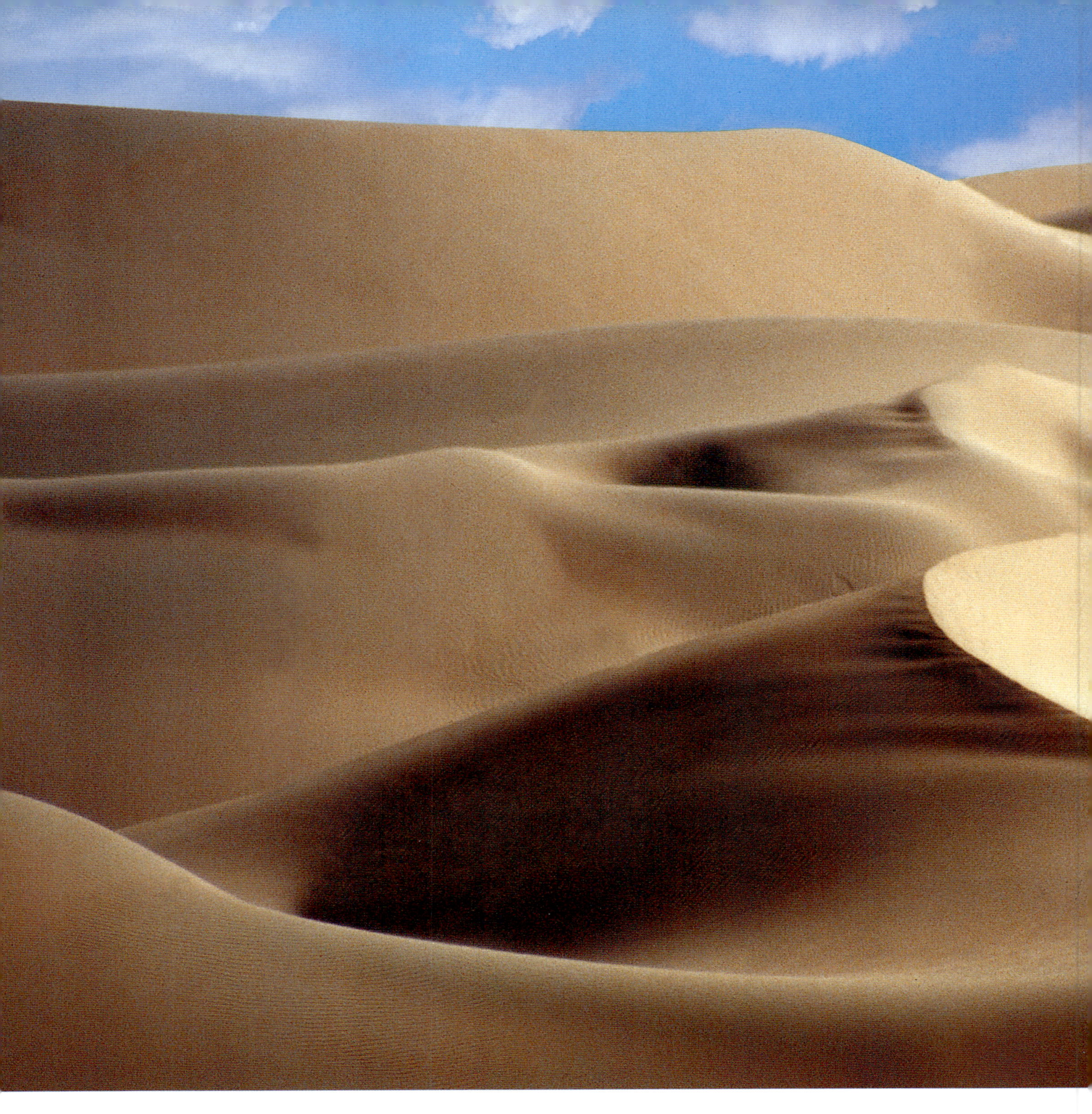

أَيَّامَ قَوْمِي خَيْرُ قَوْمٍ سُوقَةٍ   لِمُعَصَّبٍ   وَلِبَائِسٍ   وَلِعَانِي

وَلَنِعْمَ أَيْسَارُ الجَزُورِ إِذَا زَهَتْ   رِيحُ الشِّتَا   وَتَأَلَّفَ   الجِيرَانُ

دُرَيْدِ بِن الصِّمَّة

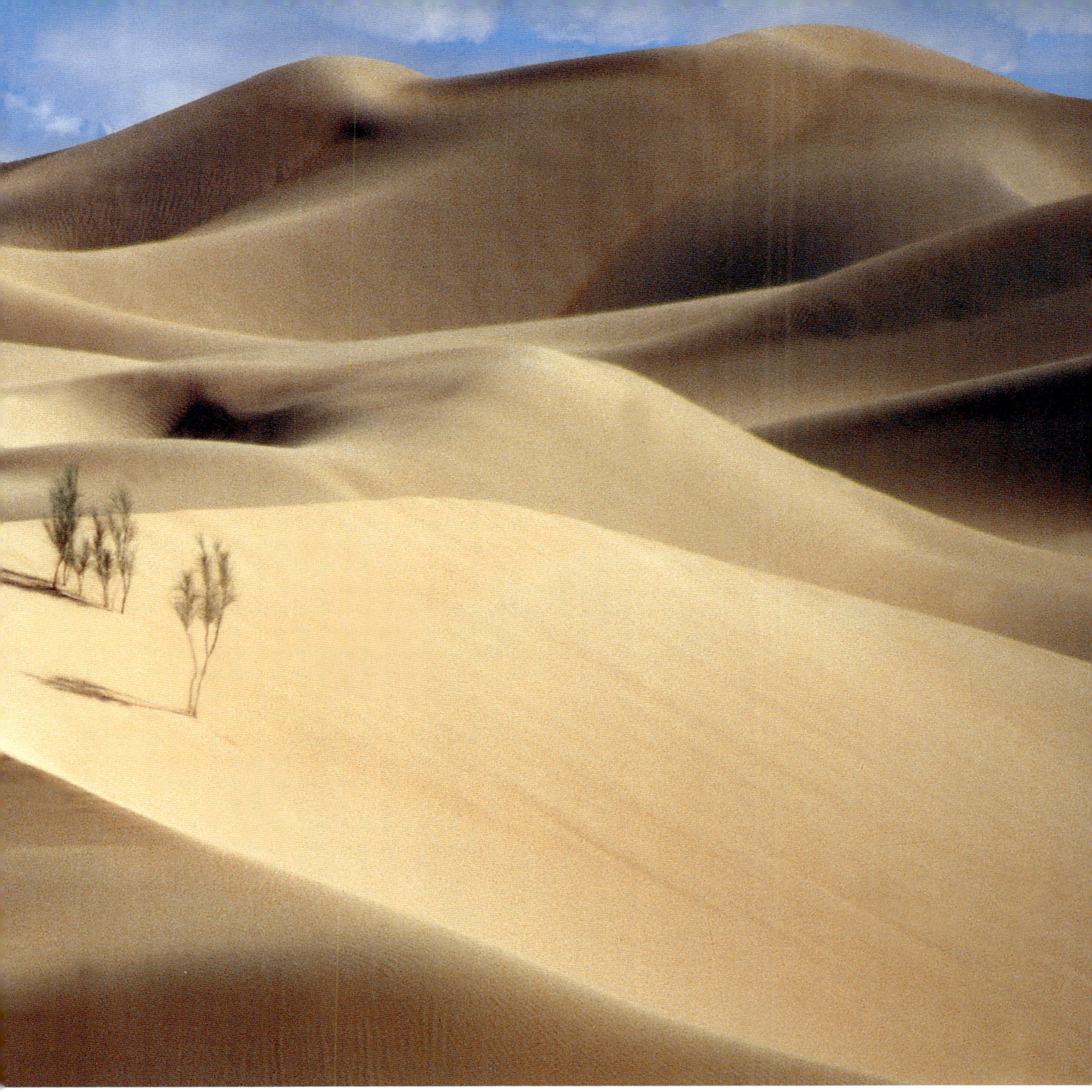

I remember the time when my people were the best of ordinary folk,
caring for those suffering from famine, hardship or imprisonment.

How excellent were those who played maysir over the slaughtered camel,
when the wind of winter blew hard and neighbours gathered together.

Durayð bin al-Simma

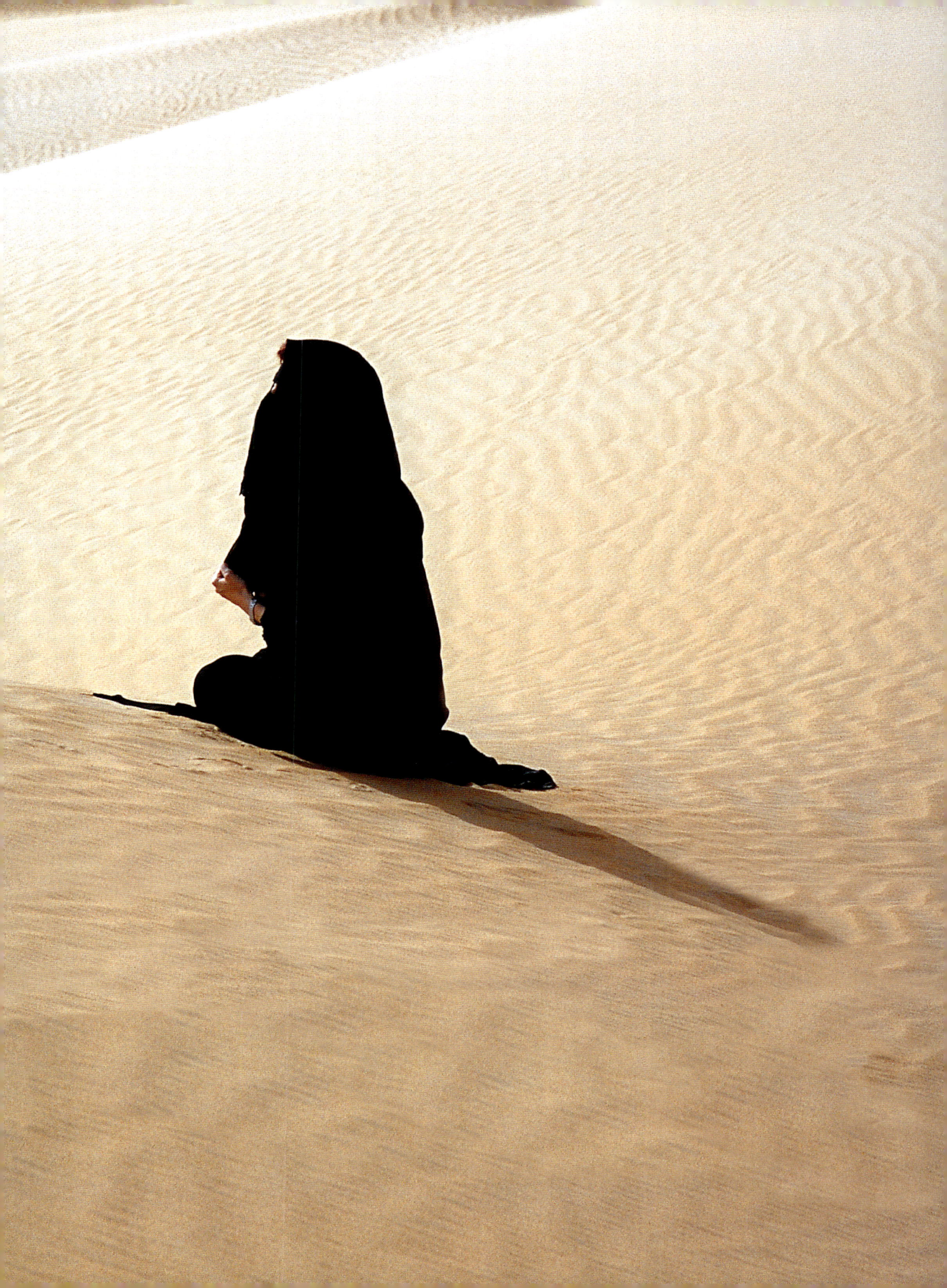

سَقَى اللهُ أَرْضًا حَلَّهَا قَبْرُ مَالِكٍ   ذِهَابَ الغَوَادِي المُدْجِنَاتِ فَأَمْرَعَا

مُتَمِّمْ بِن نُوَيْرَة

May God bring rain to the land where Malik's grave lies ~ heavy rain falling
in abundance from the morning clouds, and may He make the land verdant.

May He cause the torrent in the valleys, and a steady following rain
to make the soft spring herbage flourish.

Mutammim bin Nuwayra al-Yarbuee

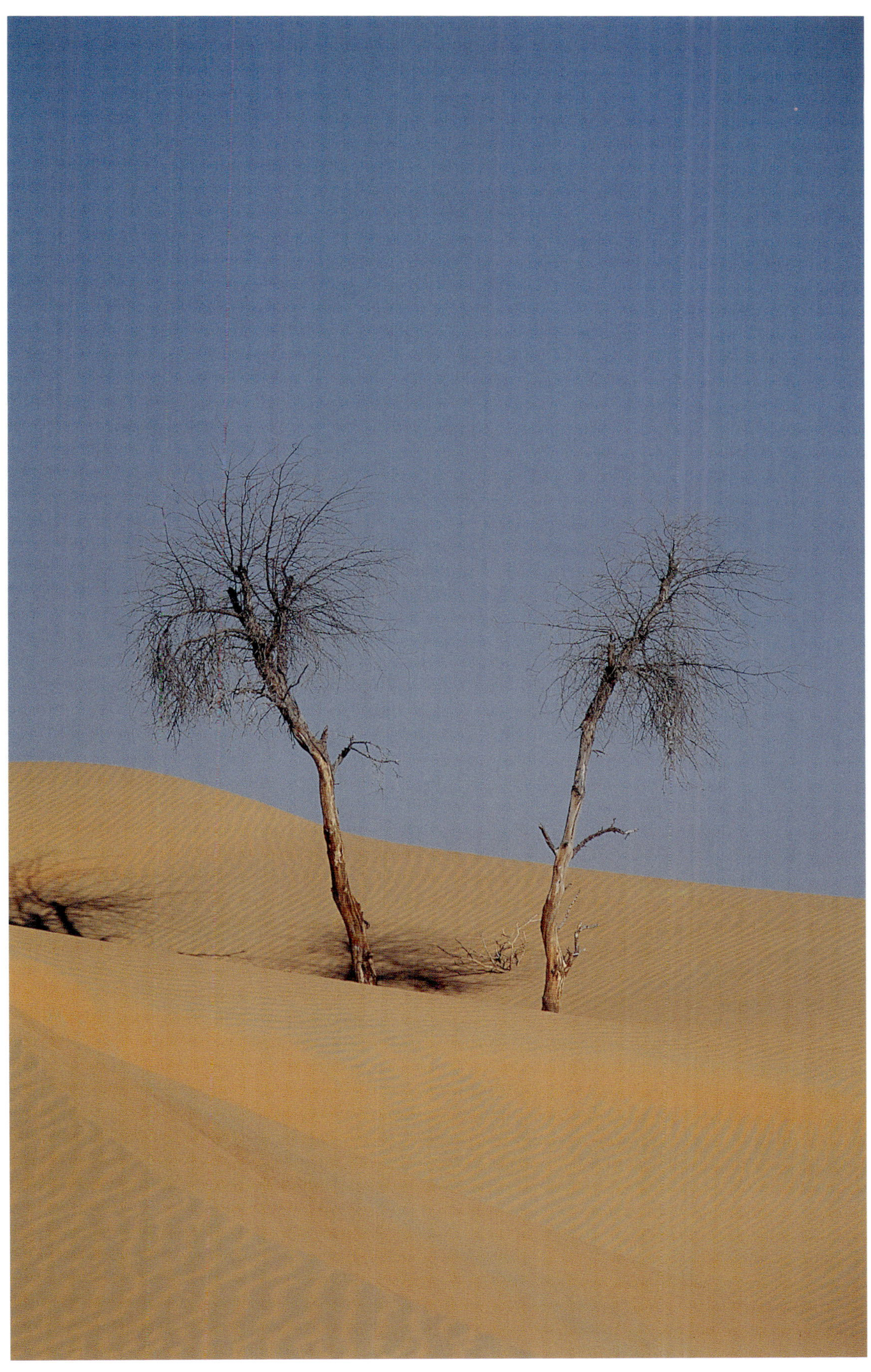

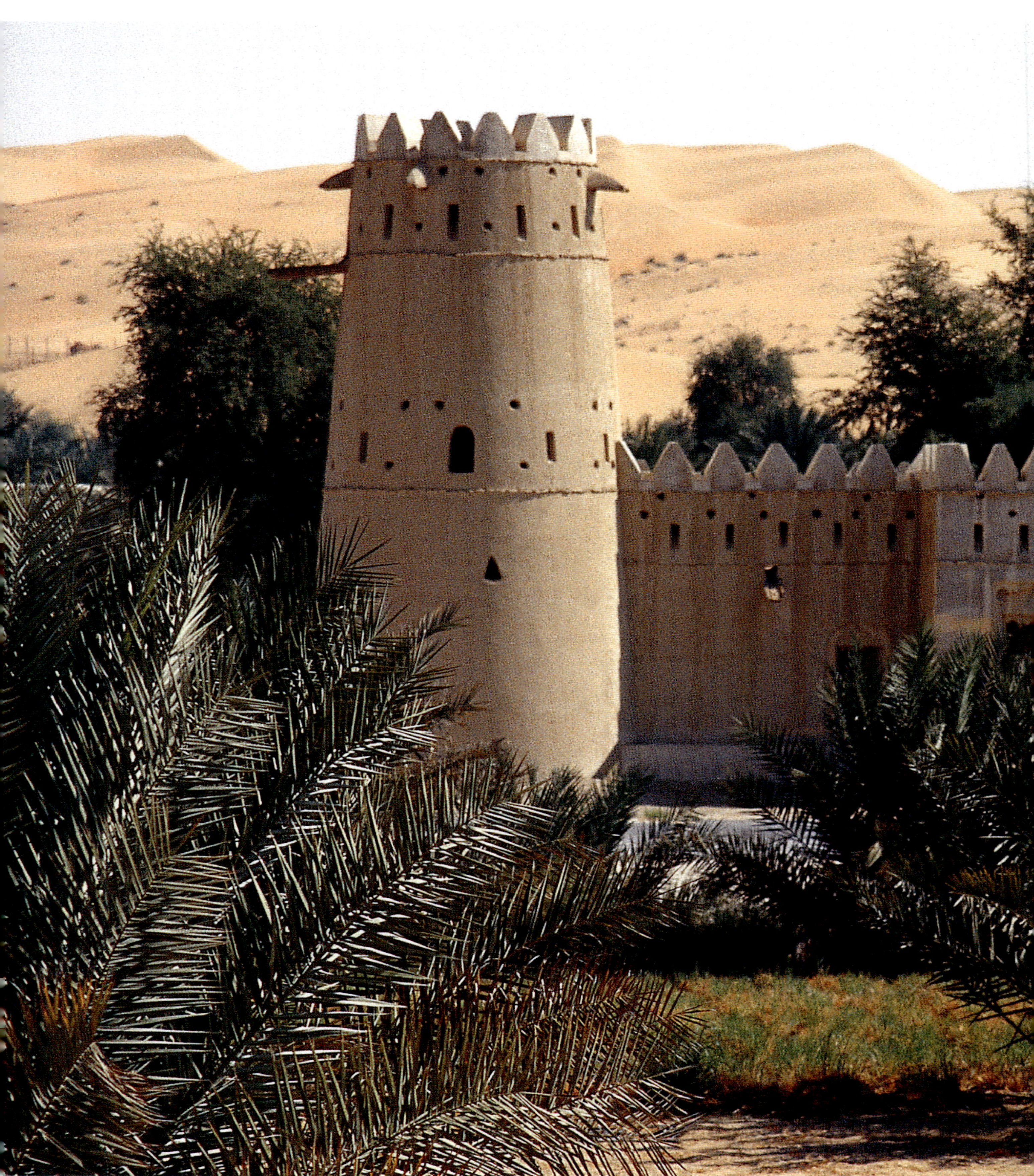

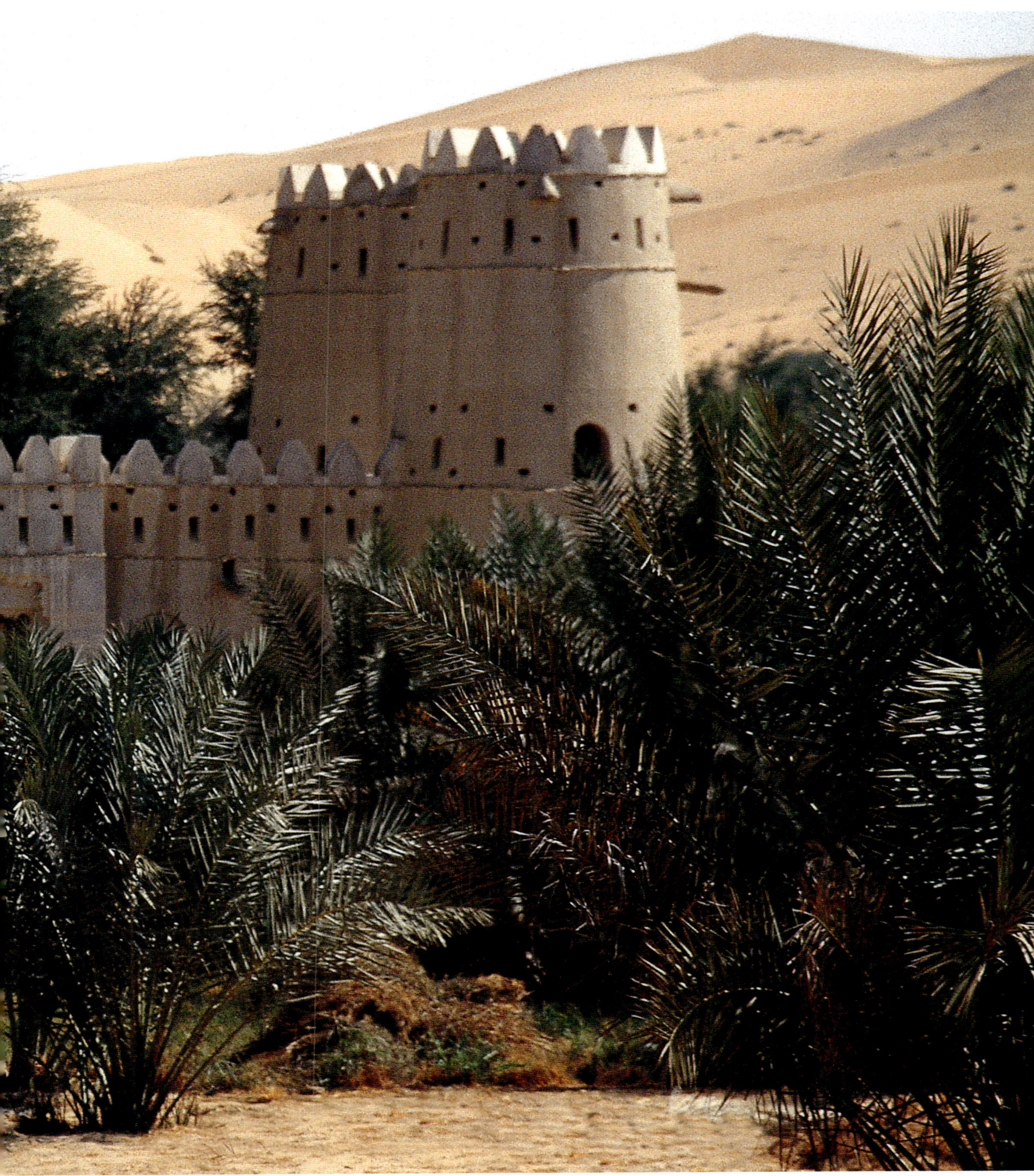

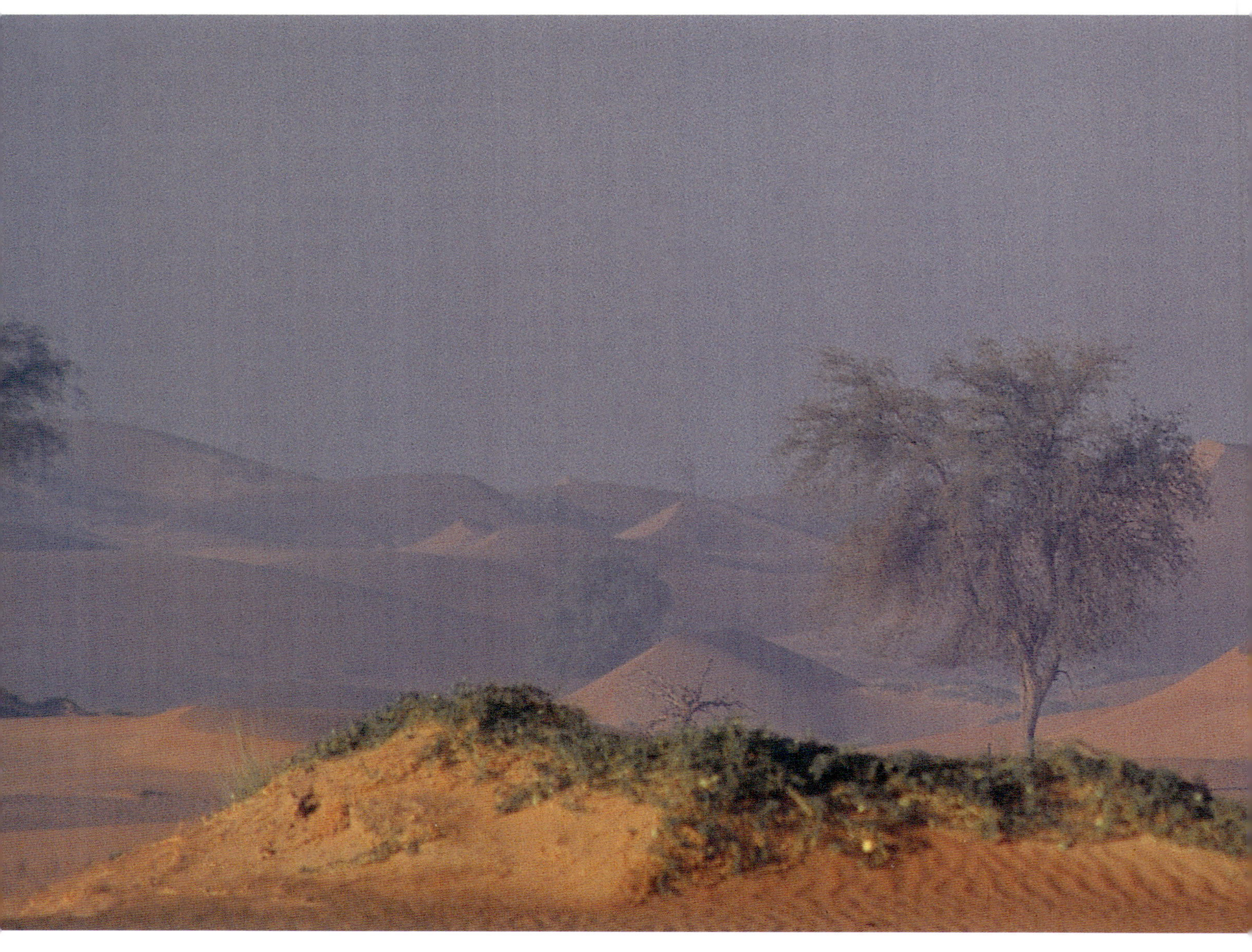

قِفَا نَبْكِ مِنْ ذِكْرَى حَبِيبٍ وَمَنْزِلِ   بِسِقْطِ اللِّوَى بَيْنَ الدَّخُولِ فَحَوْمَلِ
فَتُوضِحَ فَالْمِقْرَاةِ لَمْ يَعْفُ رَسْمُهَا   لِمَا نَسَجَتْهَا مِنْ جَنُوبٍ وَشَمْأَلِ

اِمْرُؤُ الْقَيْسِ

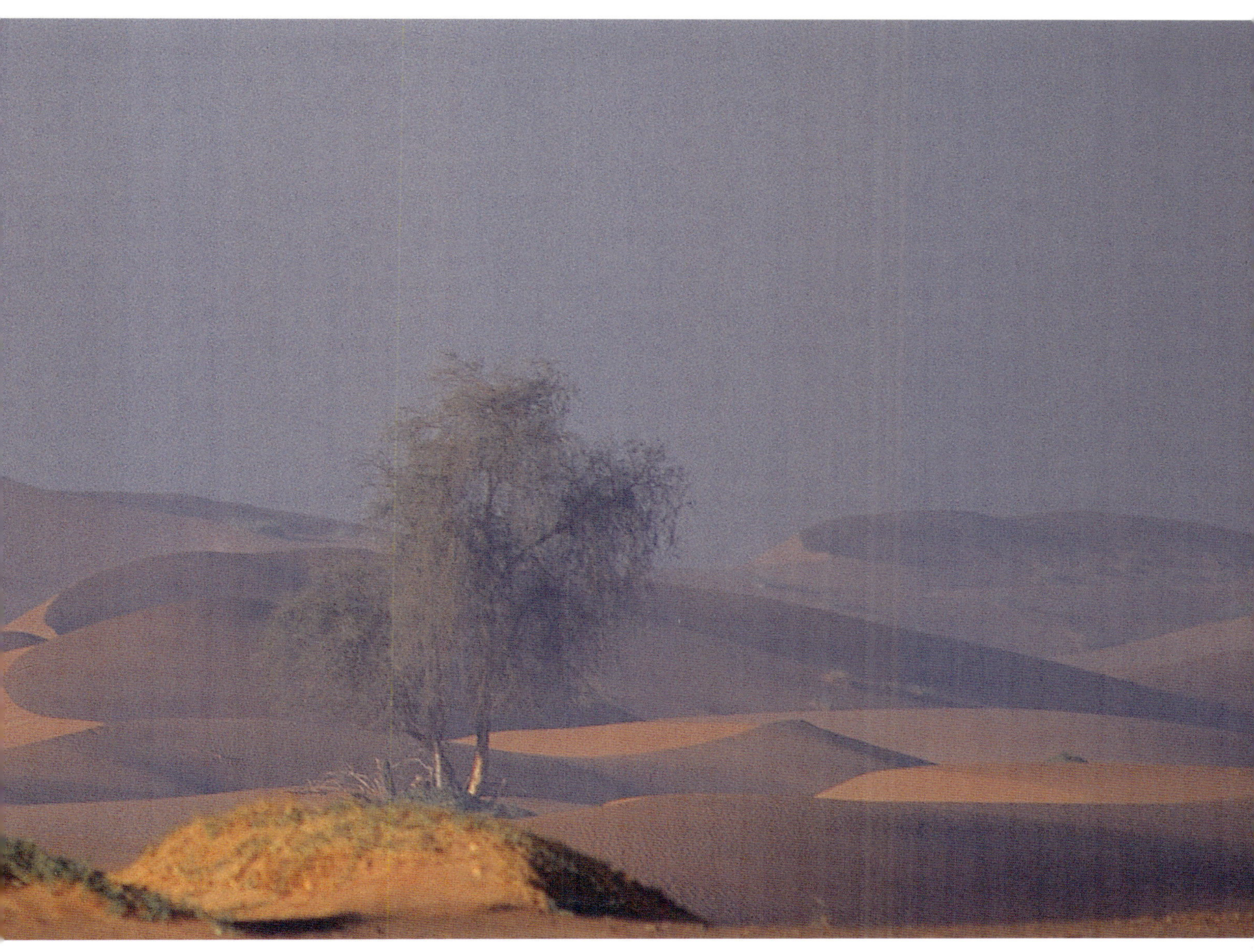

Stop, let us weep at the memory of a loved one and her dwelling,
at the place where the sands twist to an end between al-Dakhlul and Hawmal
and Tudih and al-Miqrat. Her traces have not been completely effaced,
with all the weaving of the wind from the South and North.

Imru' ul-Qays

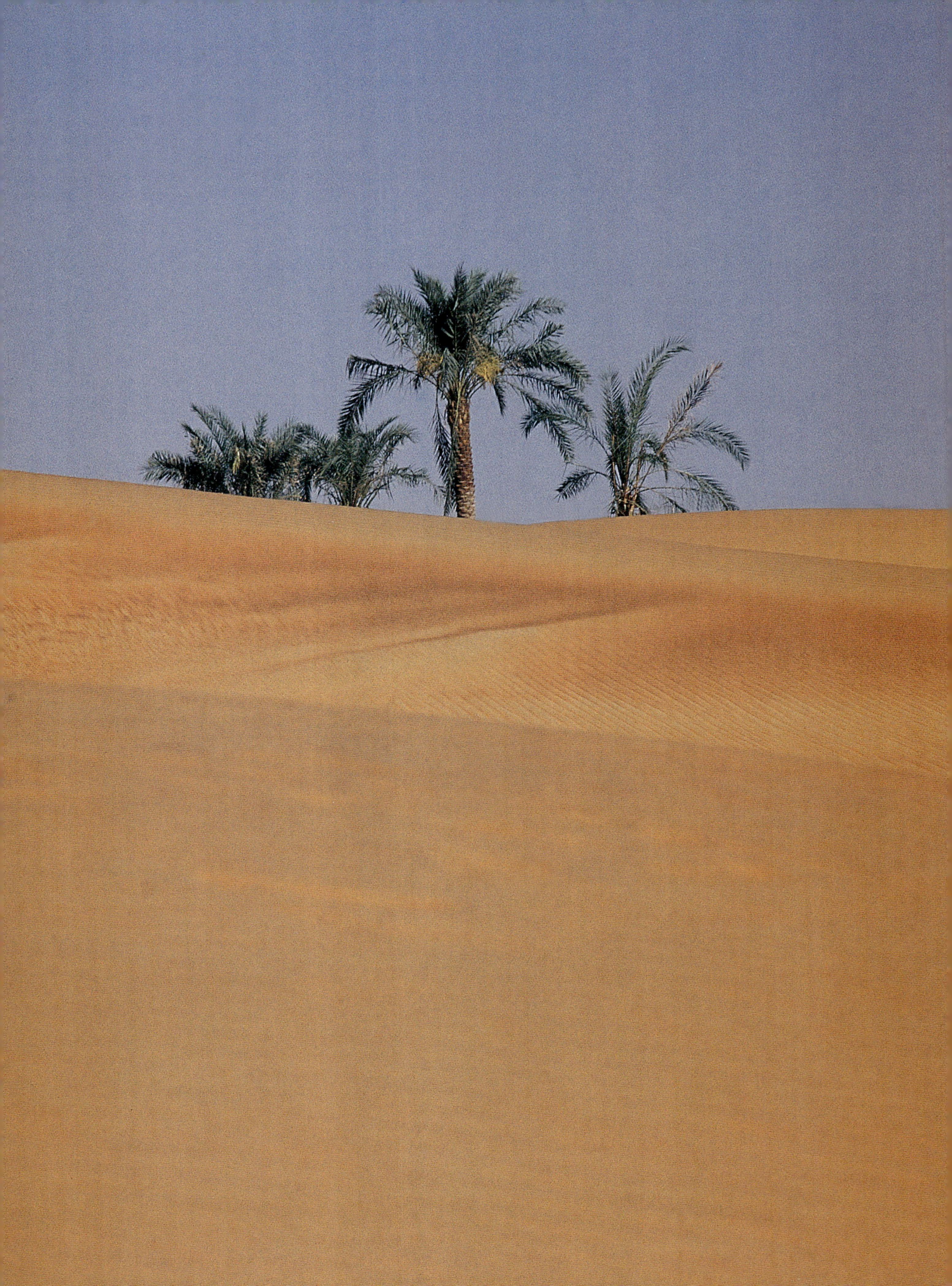

فَضَجَّ وَضَجَّتْ بِالبَرَاحِ كَأَنَّهَا وَإِيَّاهُ نُوحٌ فَوقَ عَلْيَاءَ ثُكَّلِ

الشَّنْفَرَى الأَزْدِي

He and all the wolves howl in the open desert, like bereaved women
lamenting on a high place.

Al-Shanfara al-Azdi

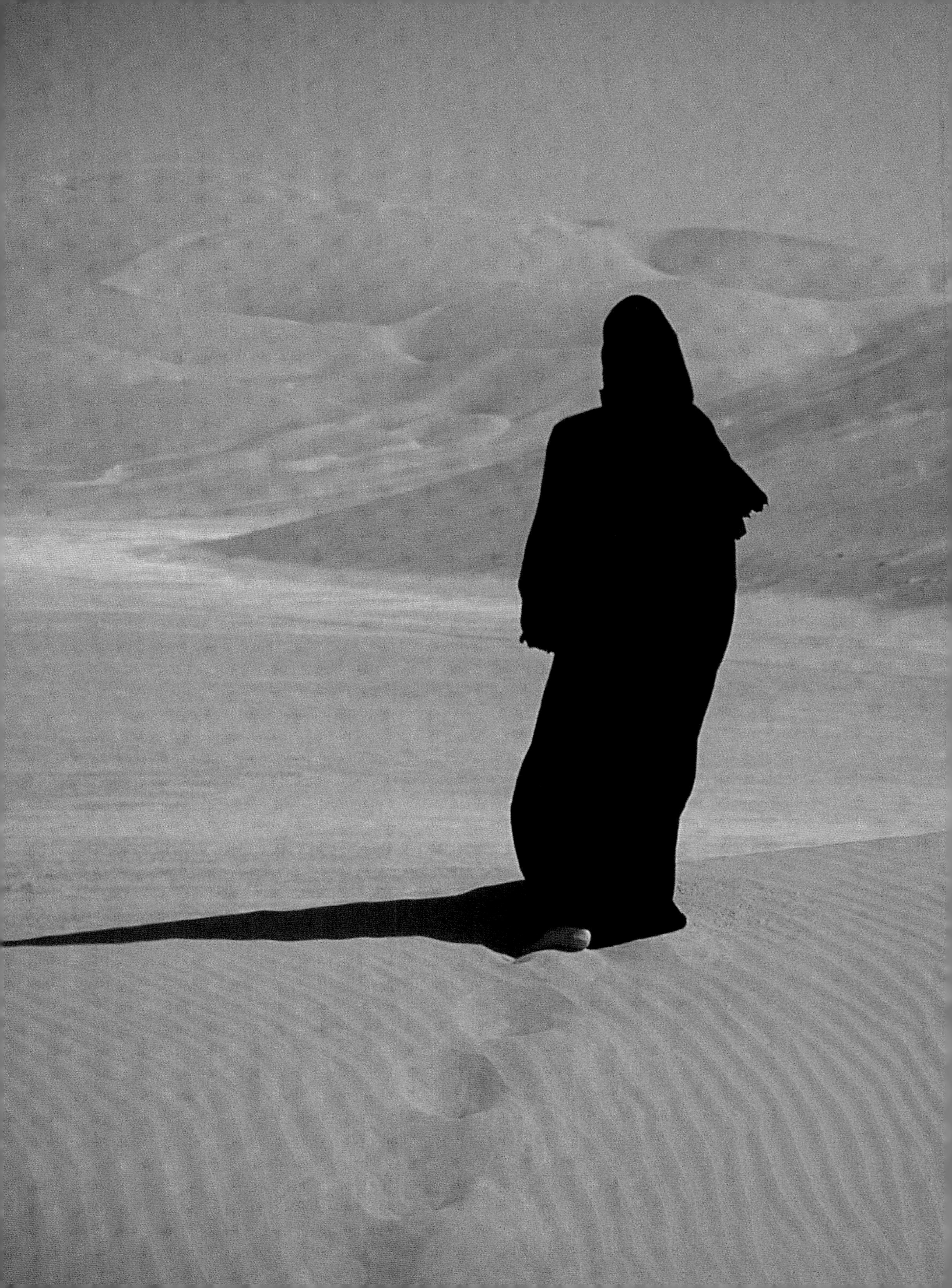

وَقُلَّةٍ كَسِنَانِ الرُمْحِ بَارِزَةٍ ضَحْيَانَةٍ في شُهُورِ الصَّيْفِ مِحْرَاقِ

بَادَرْتُ قُنَّتَهَا صَحْبِي وَمَا كَسِلُوا حَتَّى نَمَيْتُ إِلَيْهَا بَعْدَ إِشْرَاقِ

تَأَبَّطَّ شَرًّا

On many a mountain peak, pointing upwards like the tip of a spear,
exposed to the sun's rays, burning hot in the summer months,

Have I outstripped my companions ~ themselves no laggards ~
to reach the topmost point while yet there was light.

Ta'abbata Sharra

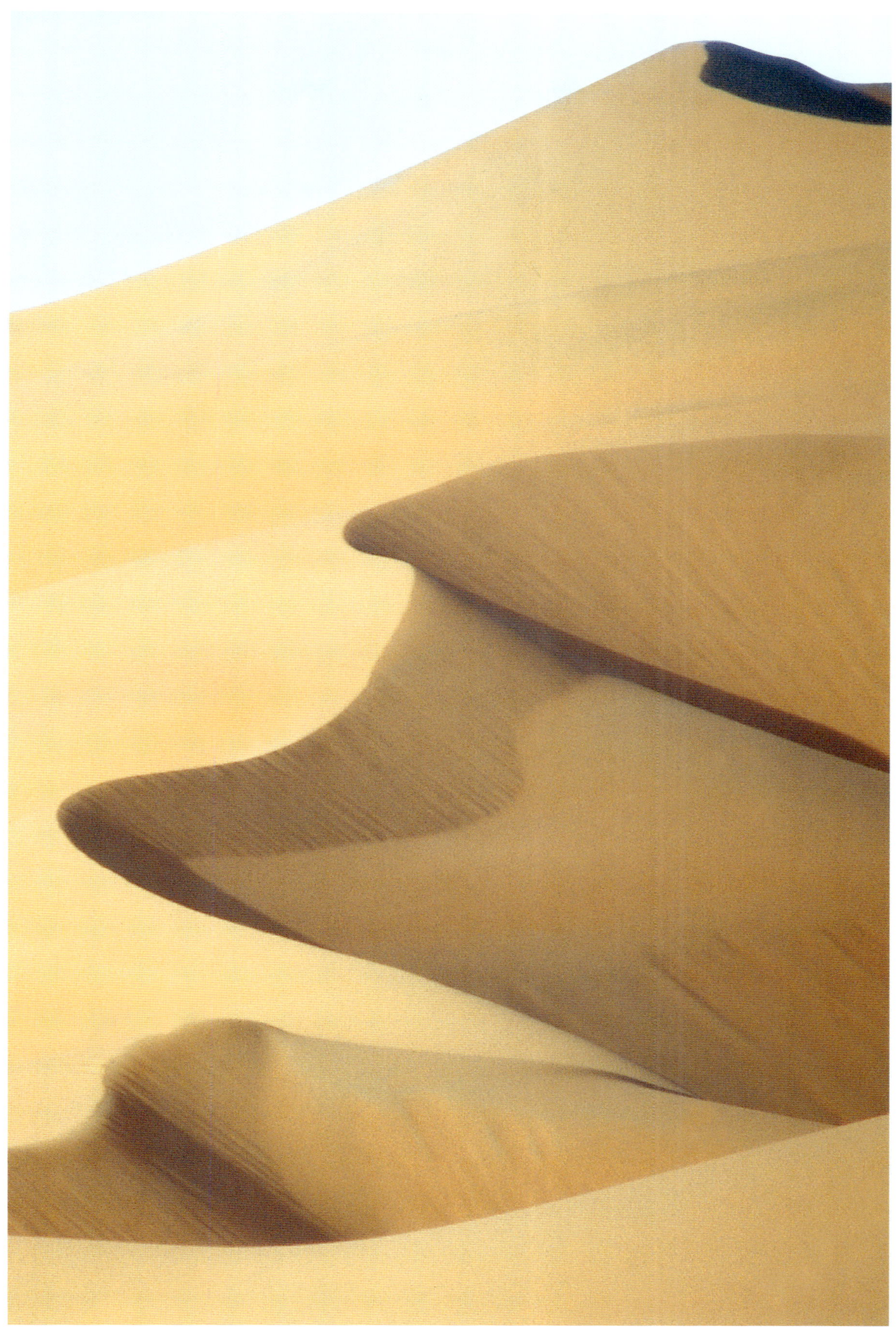

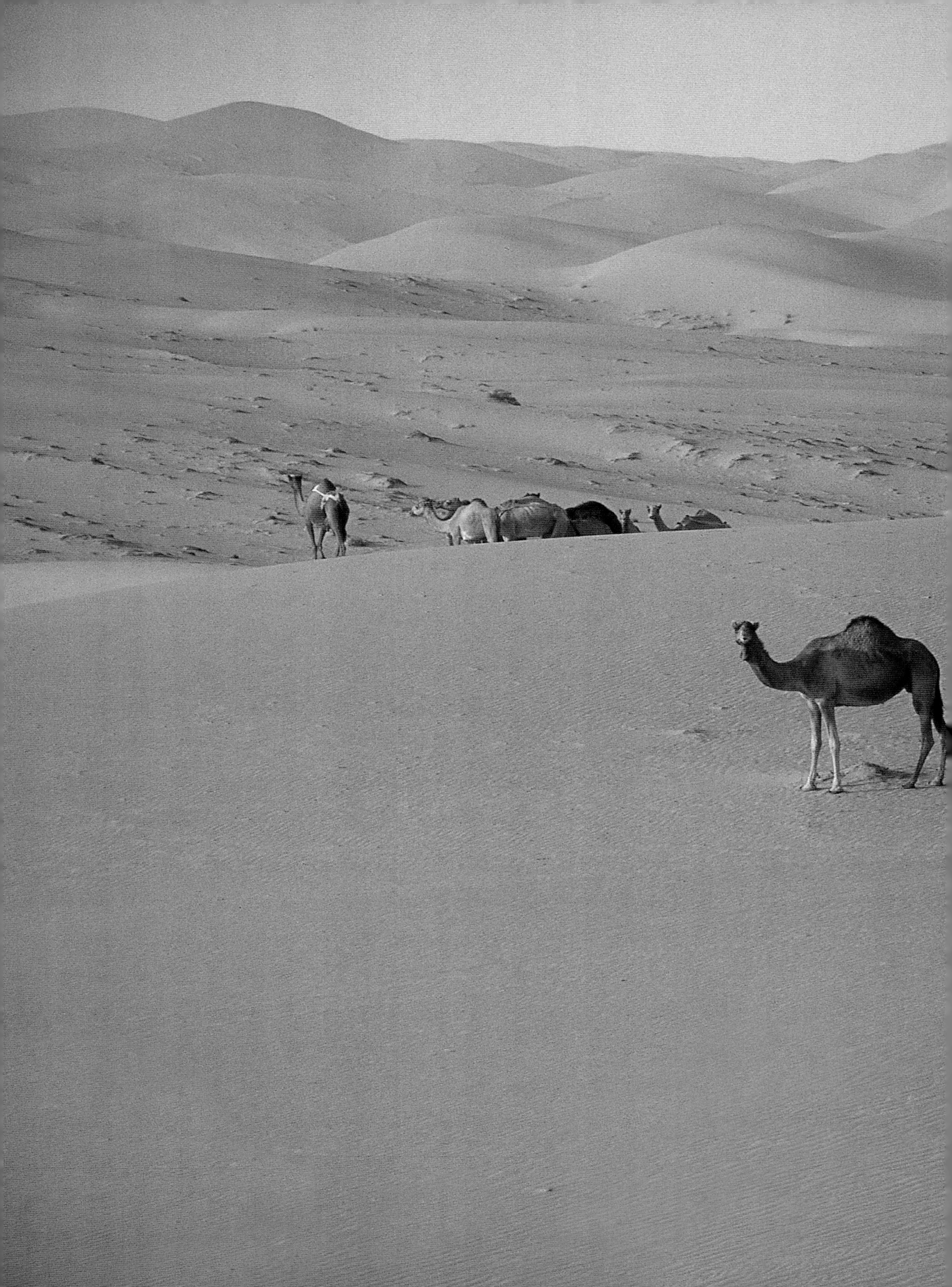

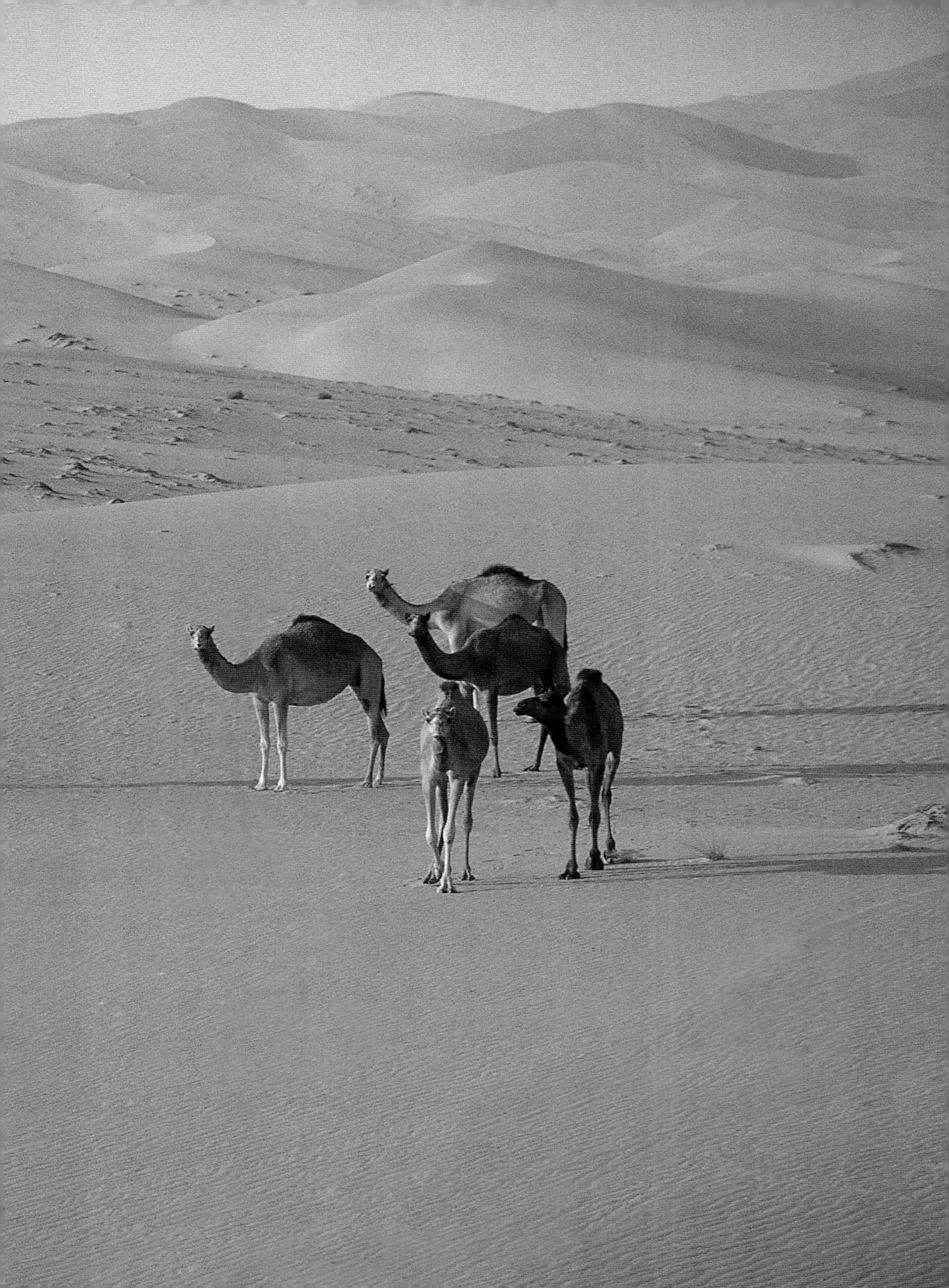

بِهِ الذِّئْبُ يَعْوِي كَالخَلِيجِ المُعَيَّلِ   وَوَادٍ كَجَوْفِ العَيْرِ قَفْرٍ قَطَعْتُهُ

قَلِيلُ الغِنَى إِنْ كُنْتَ لَمَّا تَمَوَّلِ   فَقُلْتُ لَهُ لَمَّا عَوَى إِنْ شَأْنَنَا

وَمَنْ يَحْتَرِثْ حَرْثِي وَحَرْثَكَ يُهْزَلِ   كِلَانَا إِذَا مَا نَالَ شَيْئًا أَفَاتَهُ

امْرُؤُ القَيْس

And many a valley have I crossed that was as bare as the belly of a wild ass,
where the wolf howls as it scavenges like a su'luk.*

And I said to the wolf when he howled,
'If even you have found nothing to eat, our state is one of little substance,
even as we find sustenance, it slips away from us.
Whoever tills your tilth and mine will find lean pickings.'

Imru' ul-Qays

* su'luk ~ the outcast poets who roam alone.

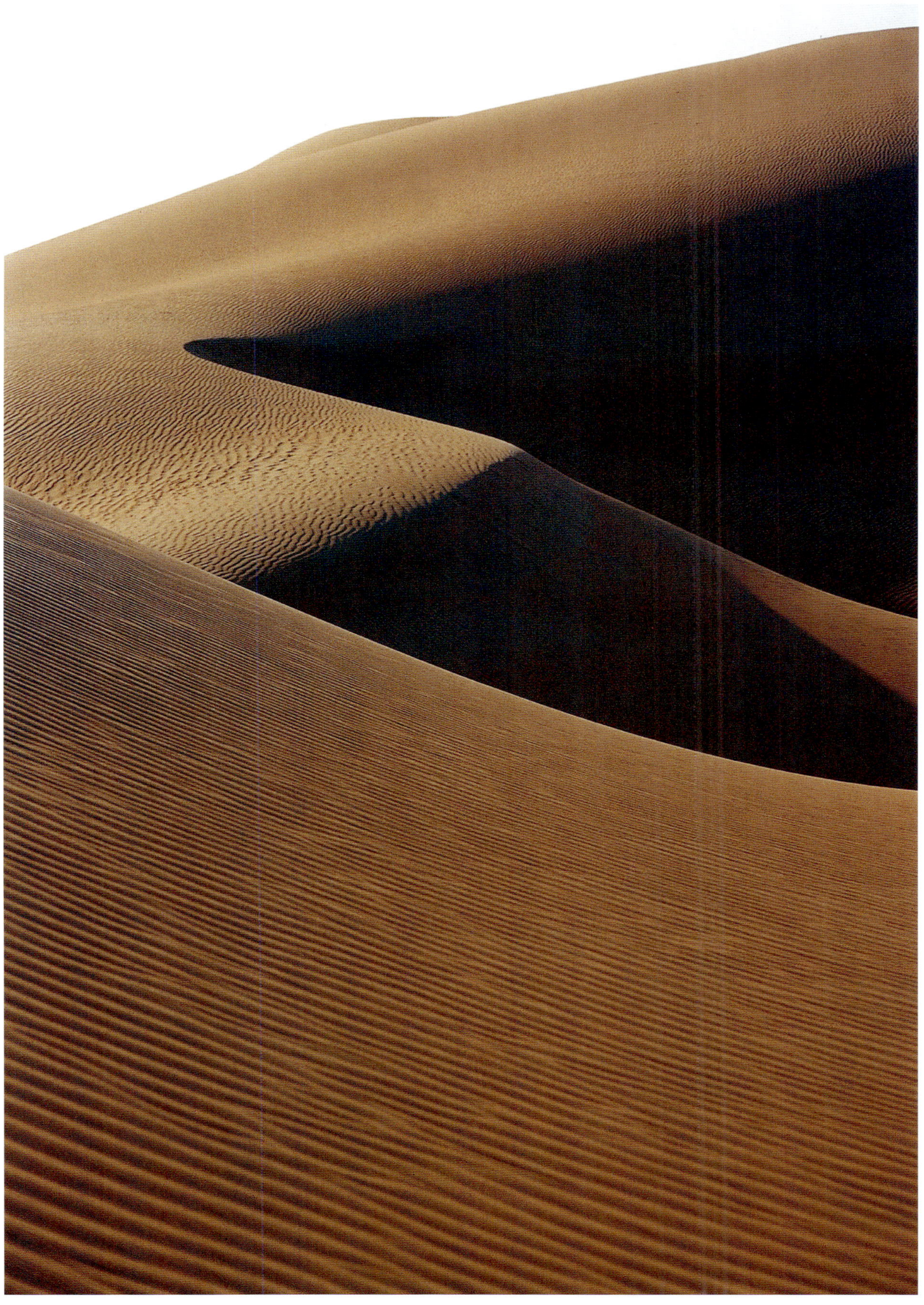

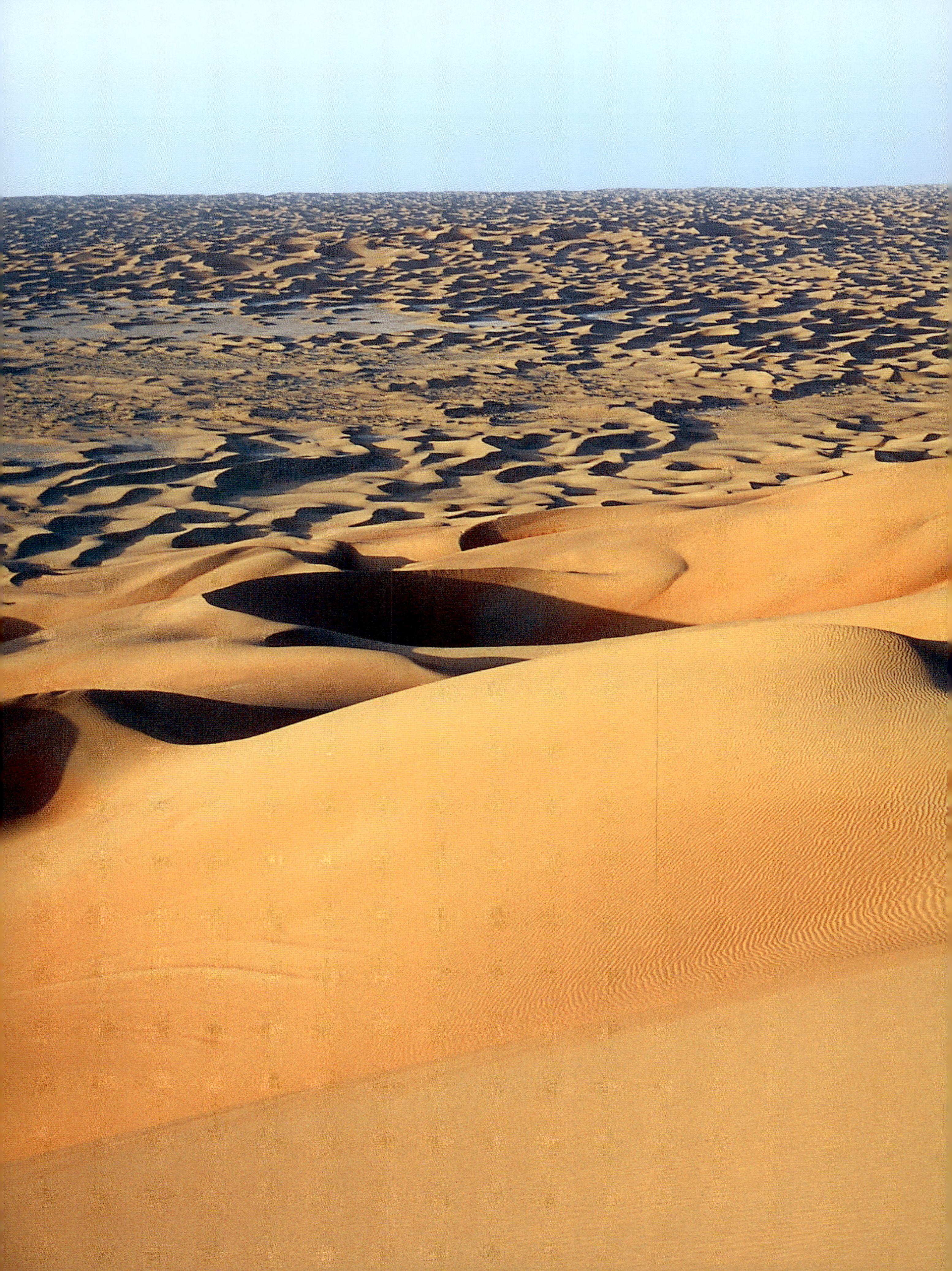

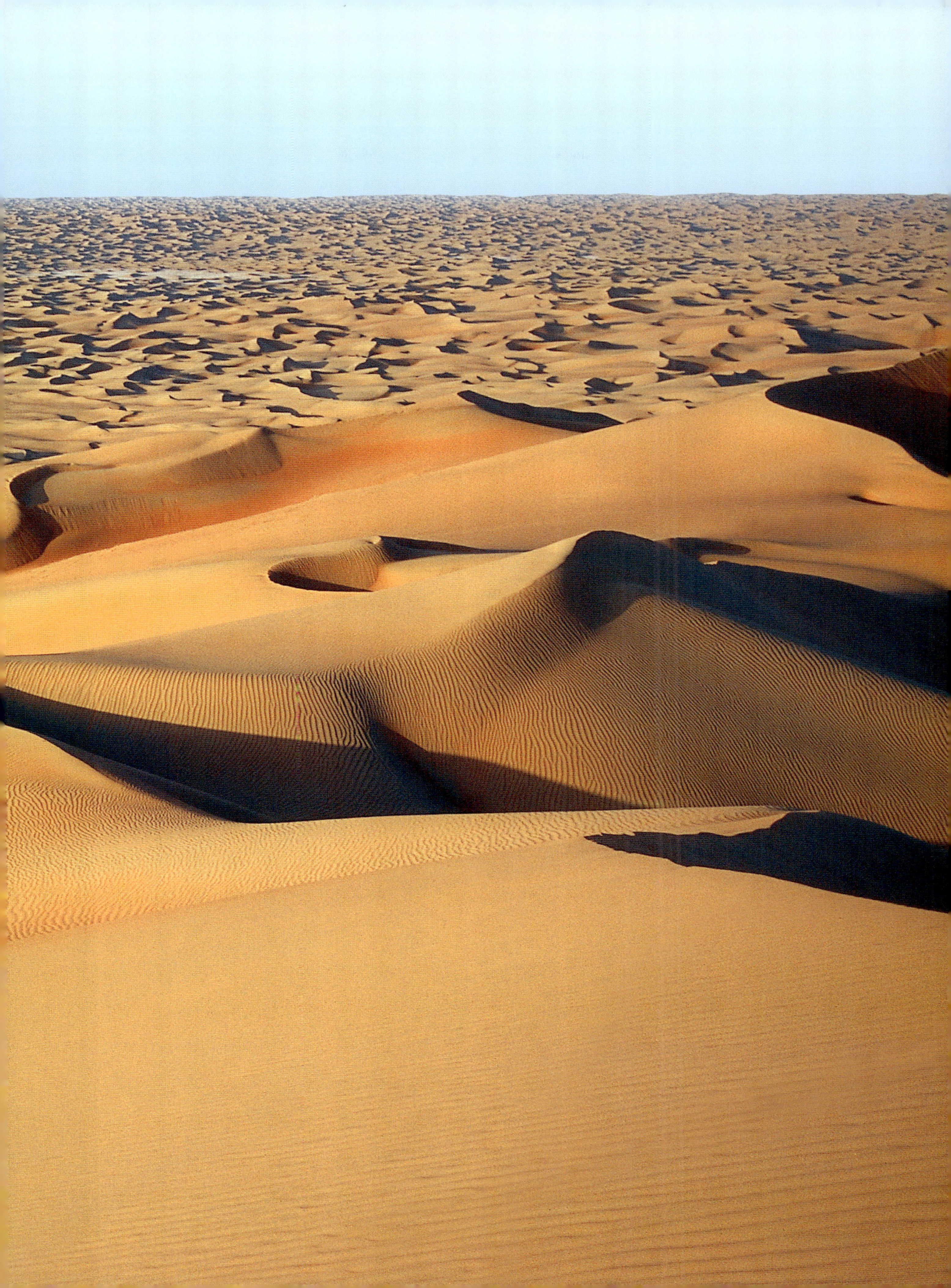

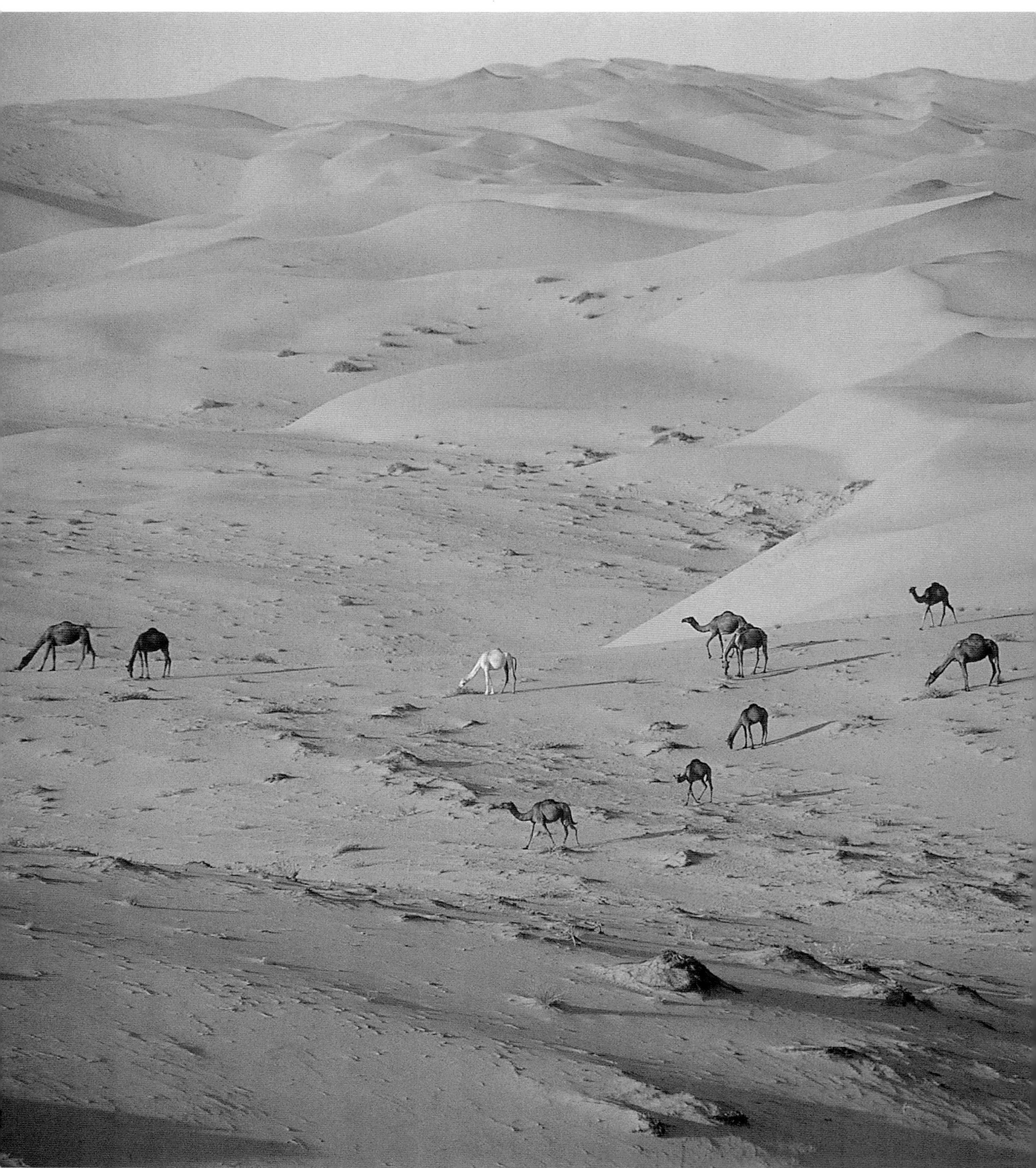

وَدَوِيَّةٍ غَبْرَاءَ طَالَ عَهْدُهَا   تَهَالَكَ فِيهَا الوِرْدُ وَالْمَرَ طَامِسُ

قَطَعْتُ إِلَى مَعْرُوفِهَا مُنْكَرَاتِهَا   بِعَيْهَامَةٍ تَنْسَلُّ وَاللَيْلُ دَامِسُ

مُتَمِّمْ بِنْ نُوَيْرَةَ

Many a dusty desert, long a wilderness, across which
the thirsty camels hasten with stones hot underfoot,

Have I crossed on a fine strong she-camel, moving swiftly,
Even when the night is dark, passing from the unknown to the known.

Mutammim bin Nuwayra al-Yarbuee

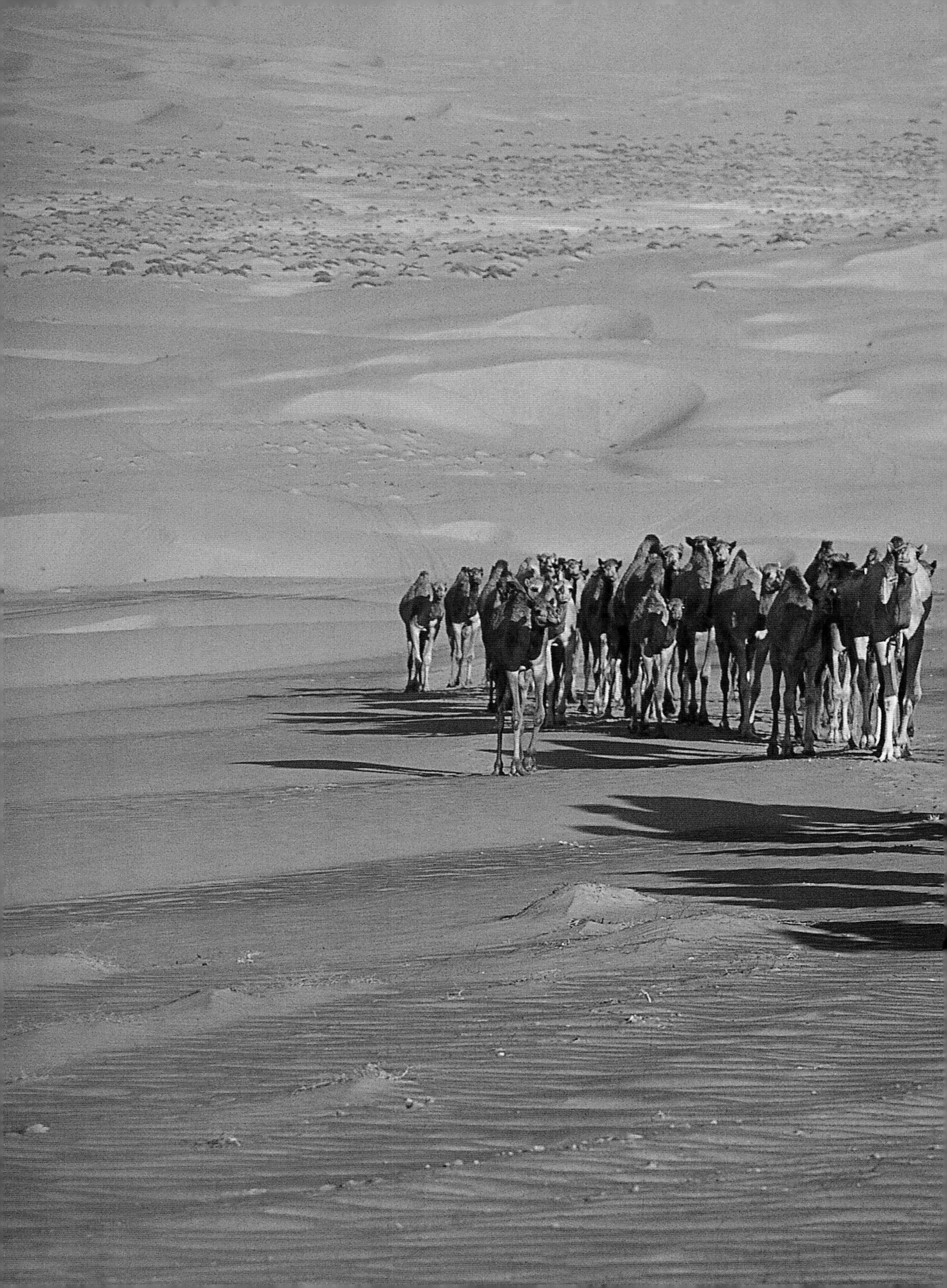

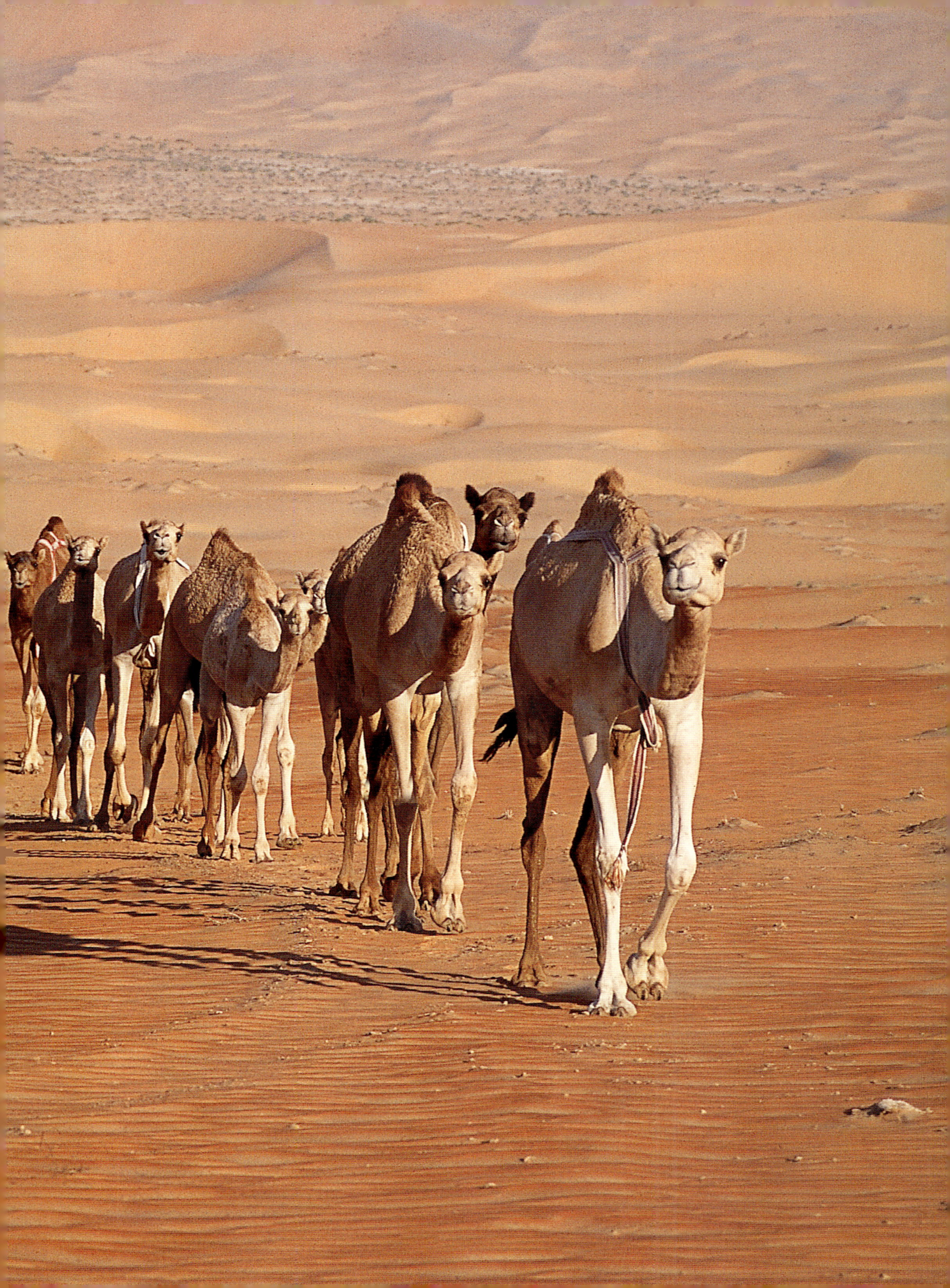

وَلَا بَرَمًا إِذَا الرِّيَاحُ تَنَاوَحَتْ   بِرَطْبِ العِضَاهِ وَالهَشِيمِ المُعَضَّدِ

دُرَّيْدِ بِن الصُّمَّة

Nor was he niggardly when the cold wind blew from different directions
on fresh branches of the thorn-trees and on dry, broken twigs.*

Durayð bin al-Simma

* Even in winter, when the wind is cold and the dead twigs snap,
the Bedouin's code of hospitality still demands generosity.

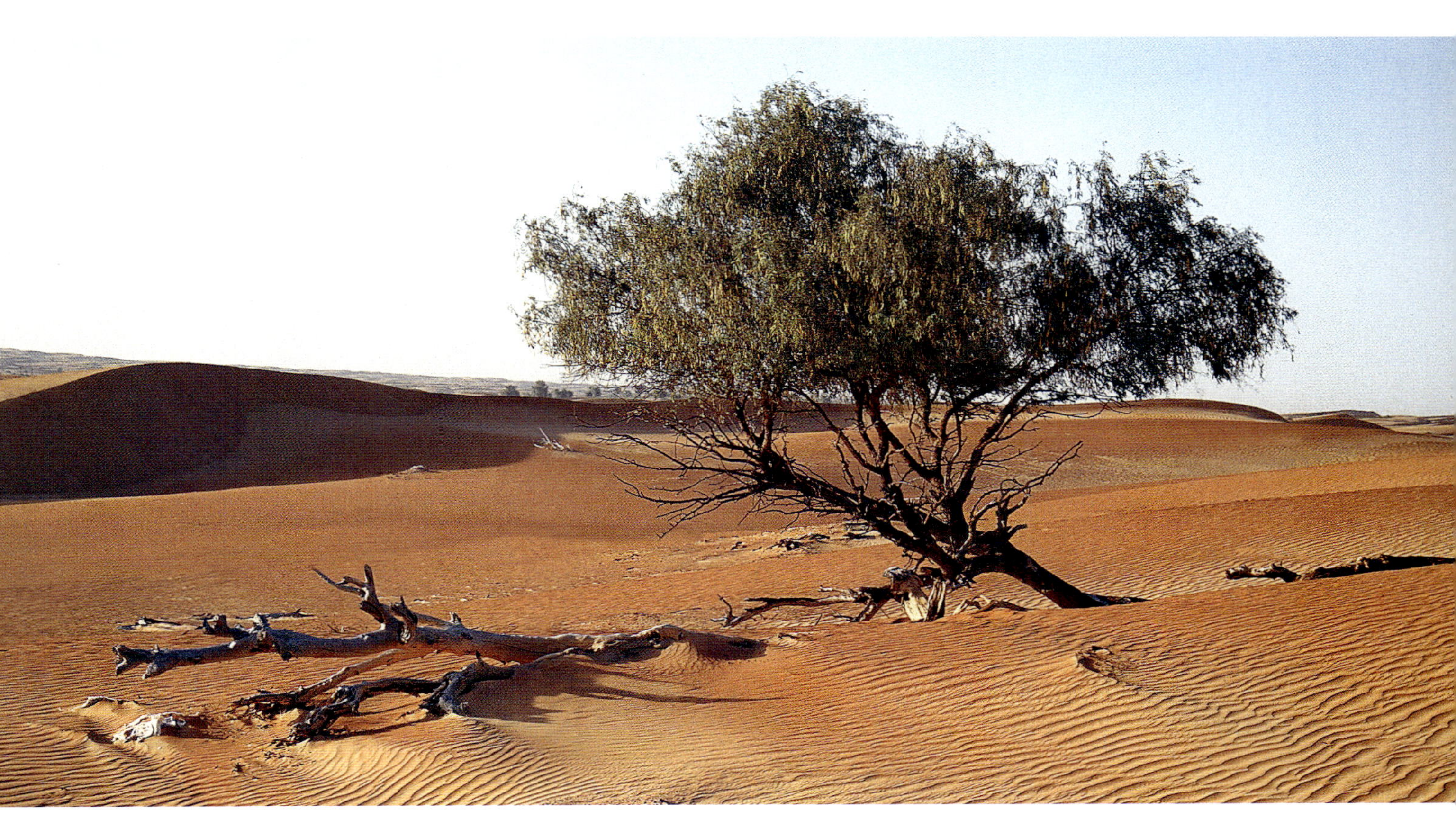

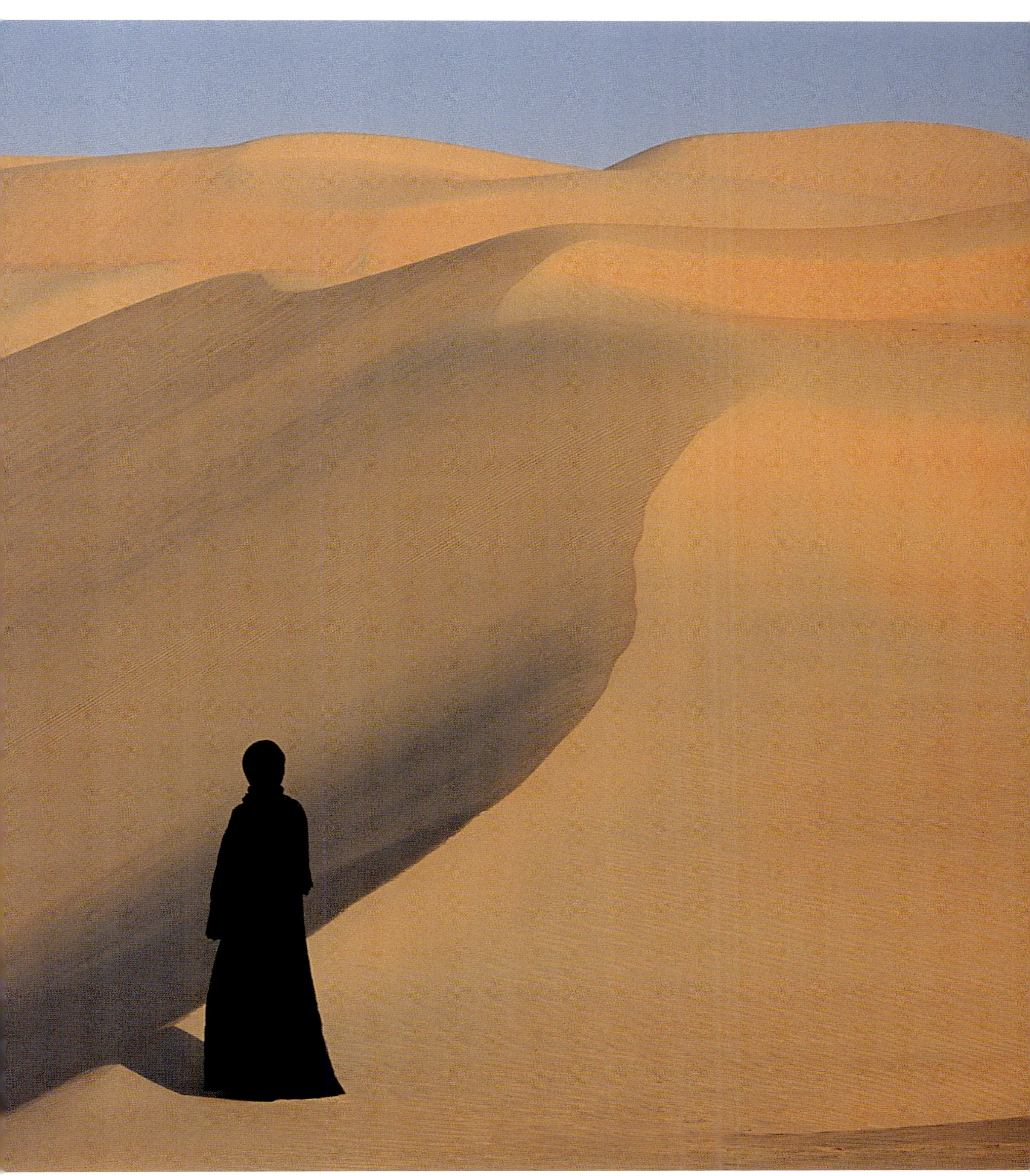

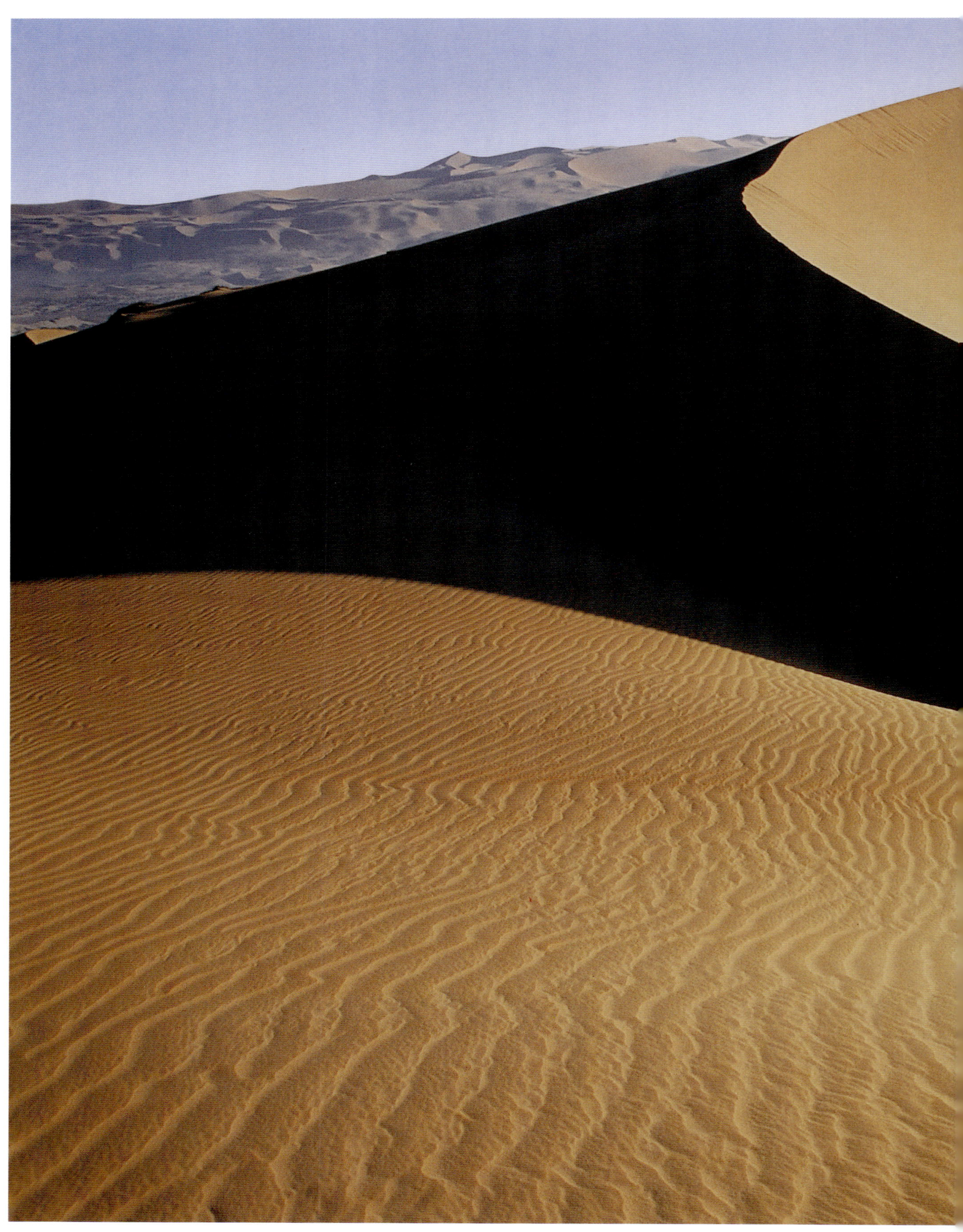

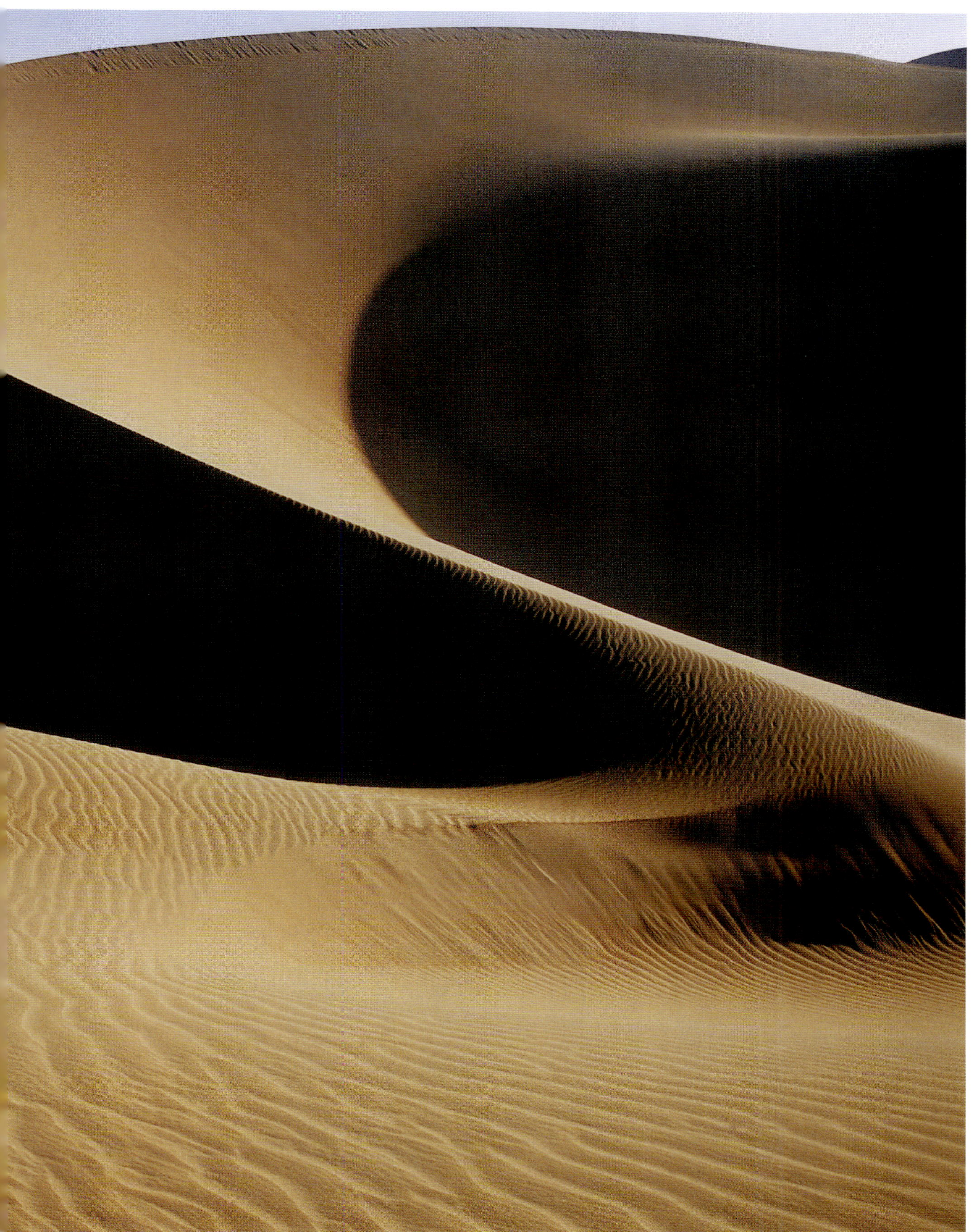

فَإِمّا تَرَيْنِي كَاَبْنَةِ الرَّمْلِ ضَاحِياً   عَلَى رِقّةٍ أَحْفَى وَلَا أَتَنَعَّلُ

فَإِنِّي لَمَوْلَى الصَّبْرِ أَجْتَابُ بَزَّهُ   عَلَى مِثْلِ قَلْبِ السِّمْعِ وَالحَزْمَ أَنْعَلُ

الشَّنْفَرَى الأَزْدِي

And if you see me going out into the midday sun like a sand snake*,
miserable and barefoot,
I have the heart of a desert cat, cloaked with endurance
and shod with resolution.

Al-Shanfara al-Azdi

* Lit. daughter of the sand.

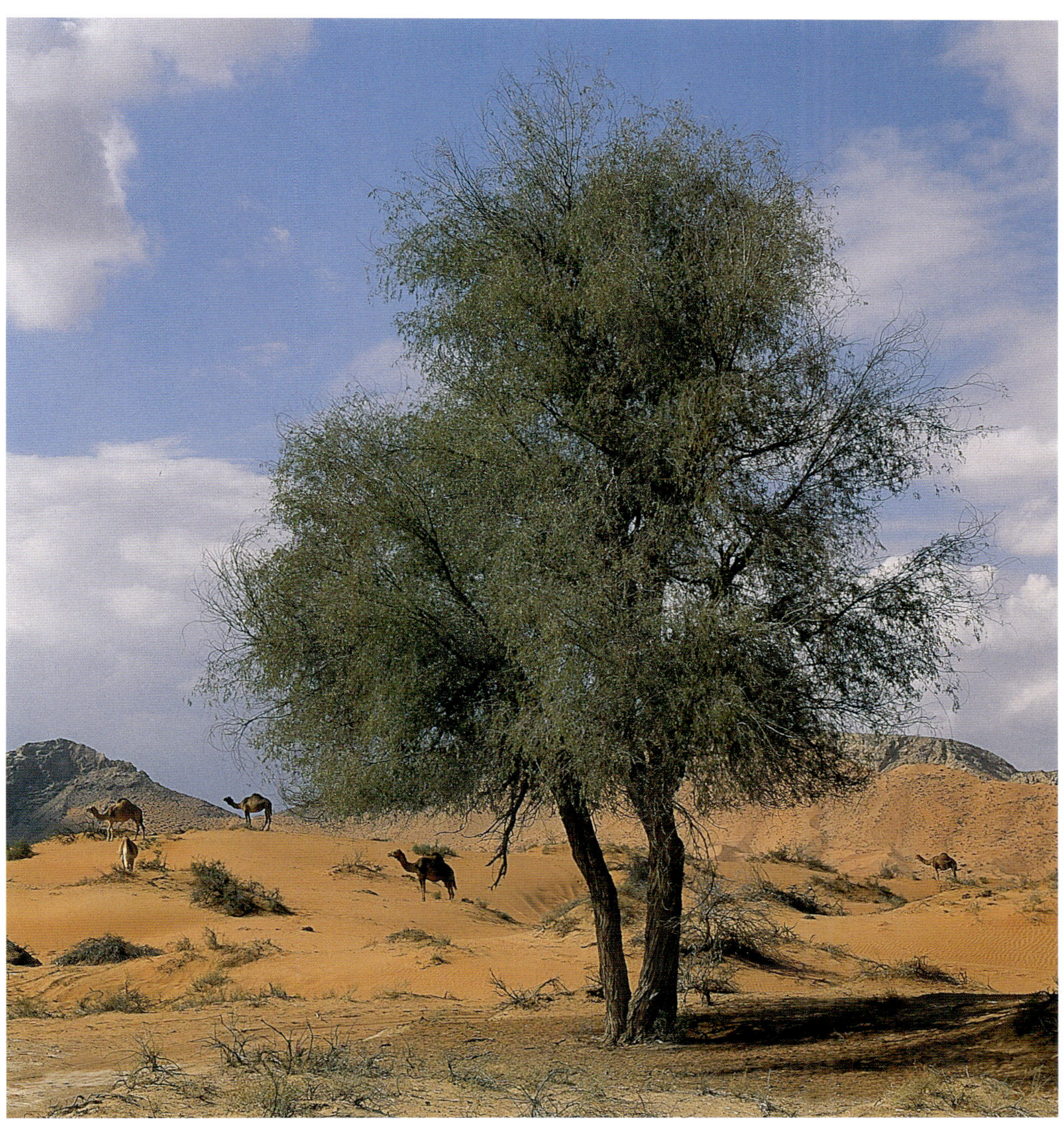

50

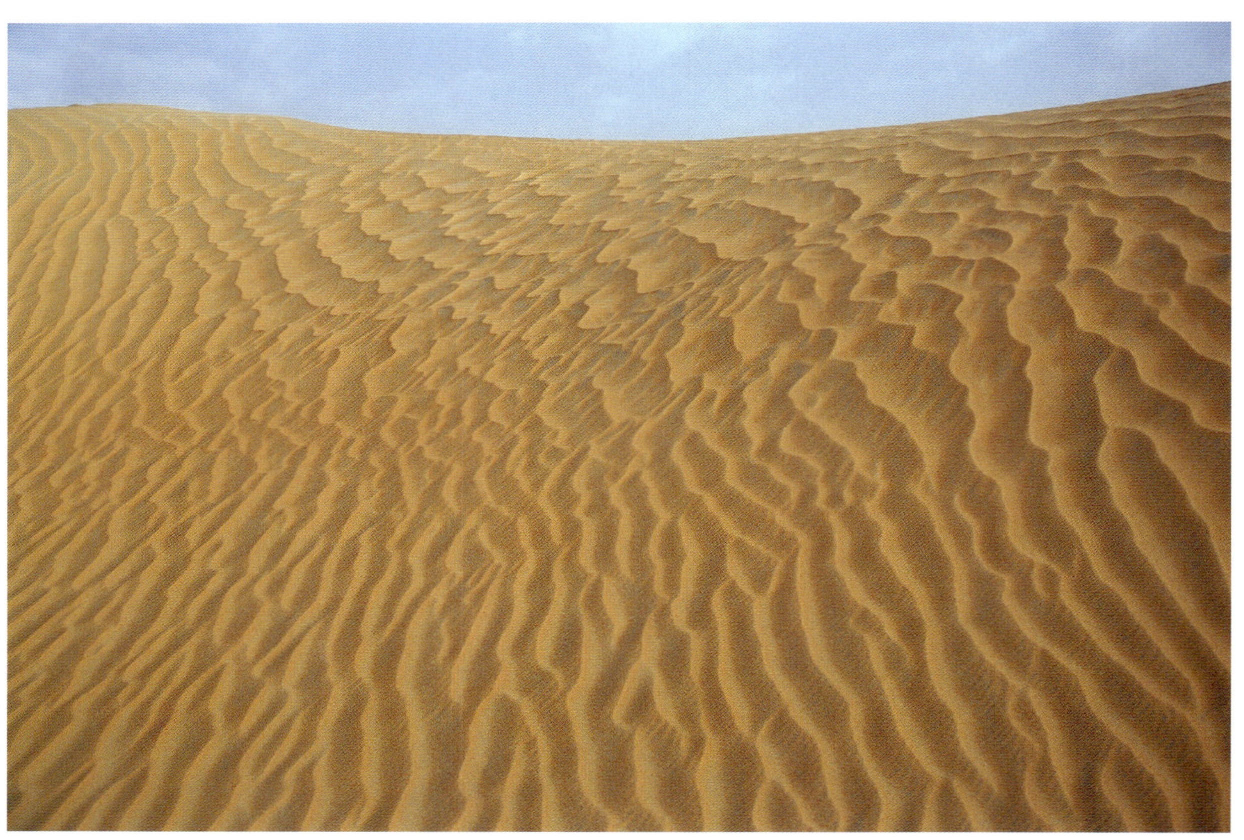

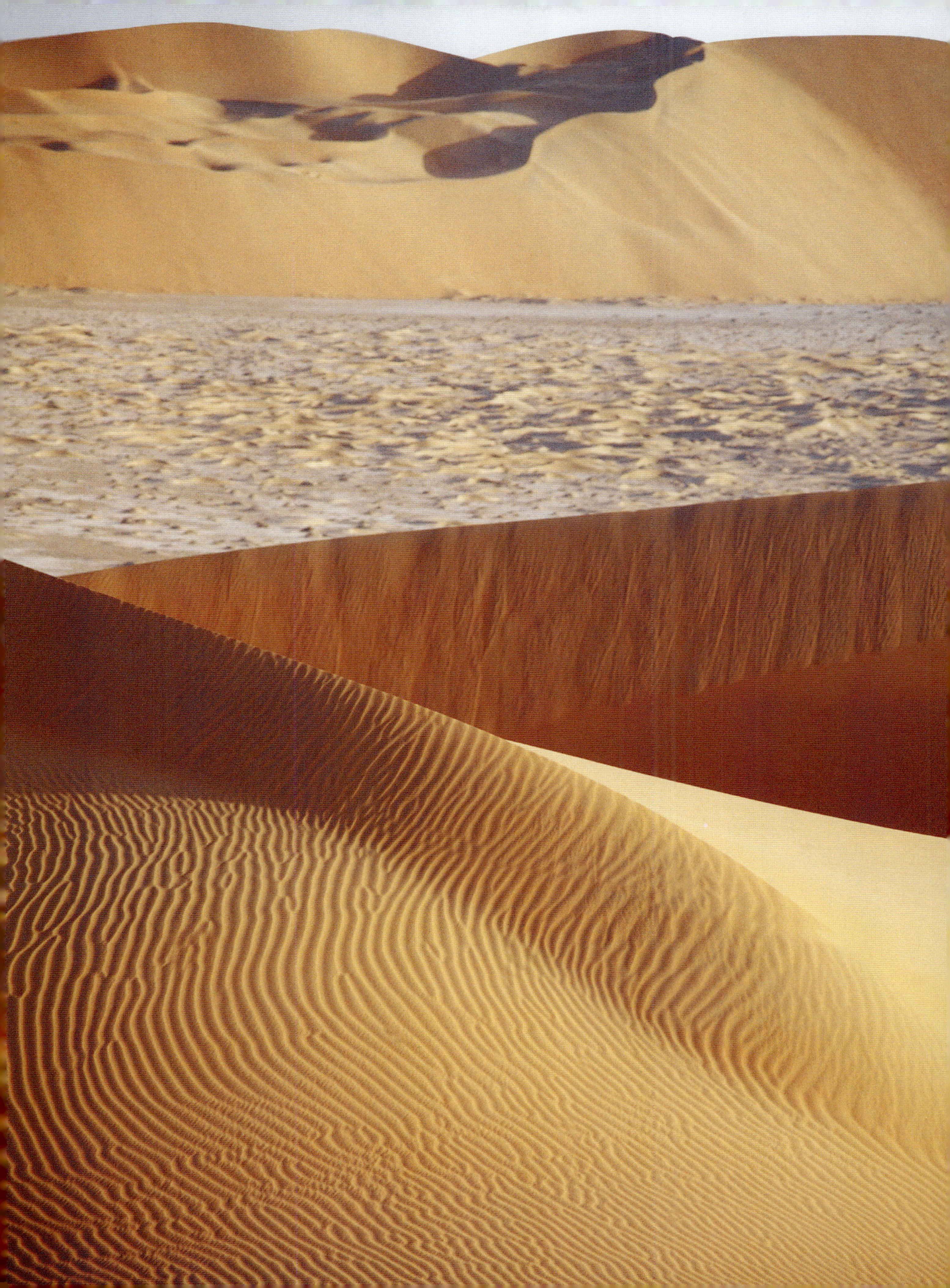

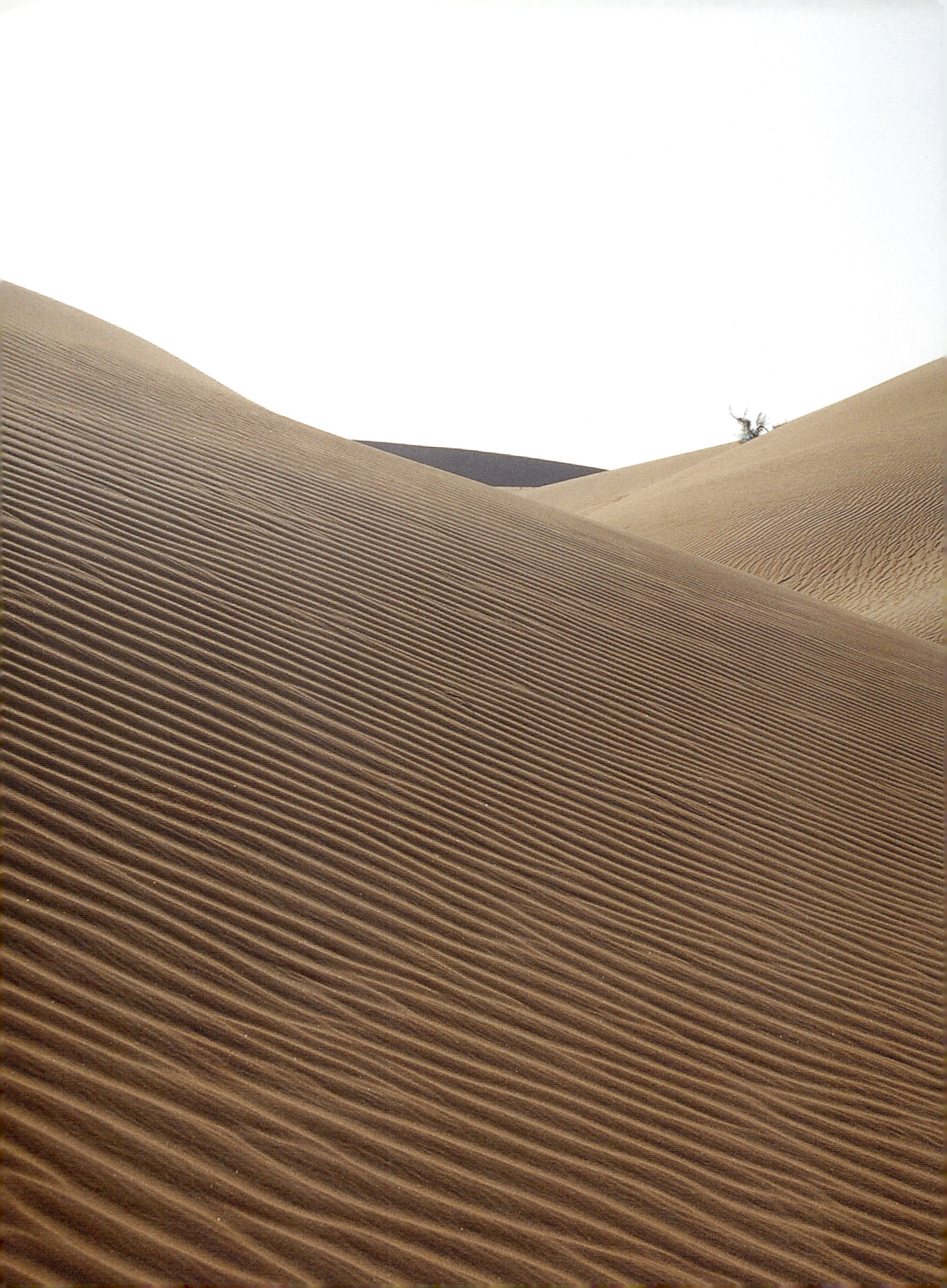

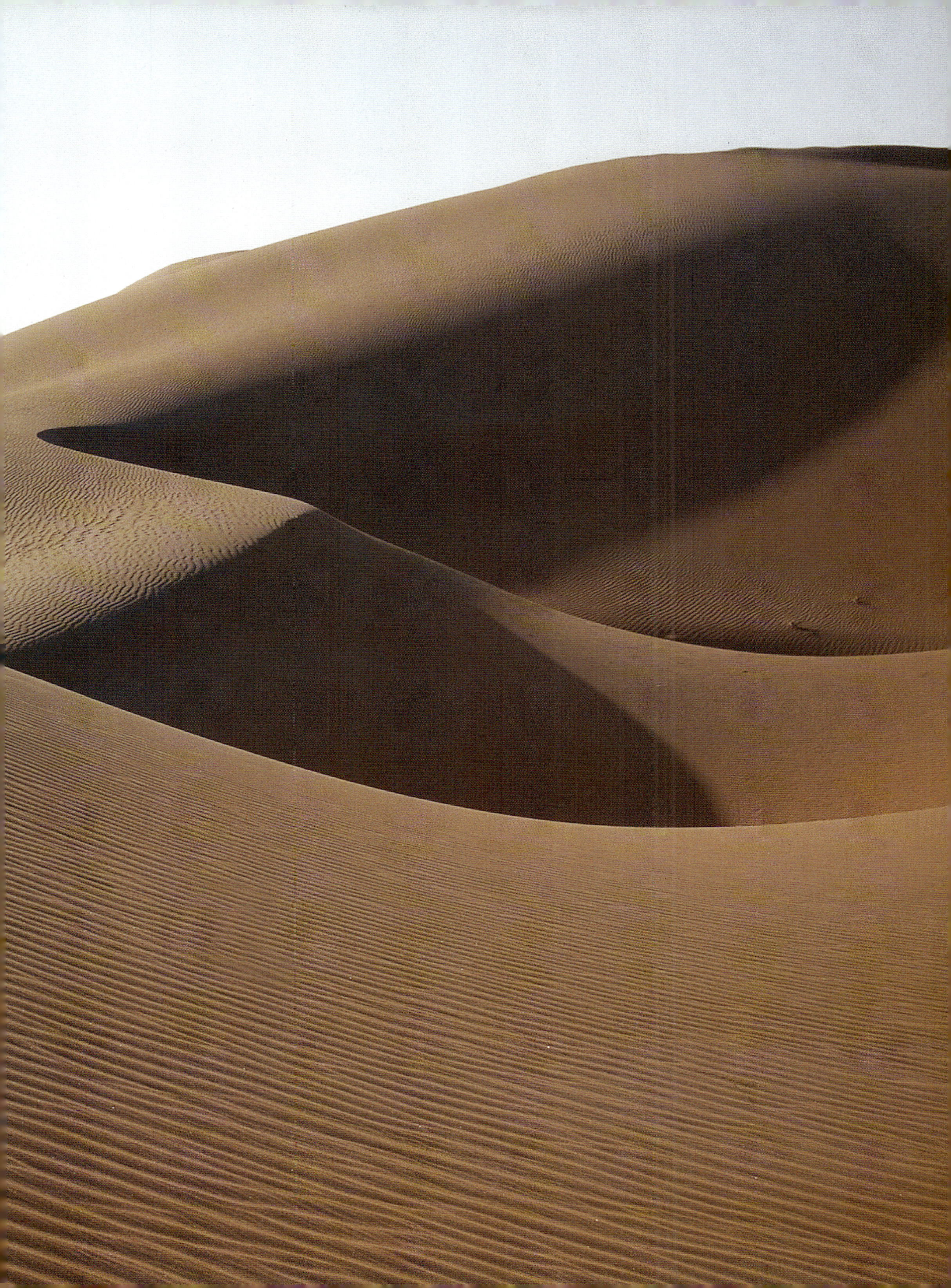

وإني قَدْ مَقيتُ الغُولَ تَهْوِي   بِسَهْبِ كالصَّحيفةِ صَحْصَحانِ

فَقُلْتُ لَهَا كِلانَا نَضْوُ أَيْنٍ   أَخُو سَفَرٍ فَخَلّي لِي مَكانِي

تَأَبَّطَ شَرًّا

Truth to tell, I met a *ghul** darting along a waterless stretch of desert,
flat and featureless like a sheet of paper.

I said to her, 'Both of us are worn out by fatigue and are ever travelling,
so leave my place free for me.'

Ta'abbata Sharra

* The English word 'ghoul' derives from the Arabic *ghul*, a mythical she-beast of pre-Islamic poetry.
Hit once, a *ghul* is vanquished; hit twice, she rises to fight again.

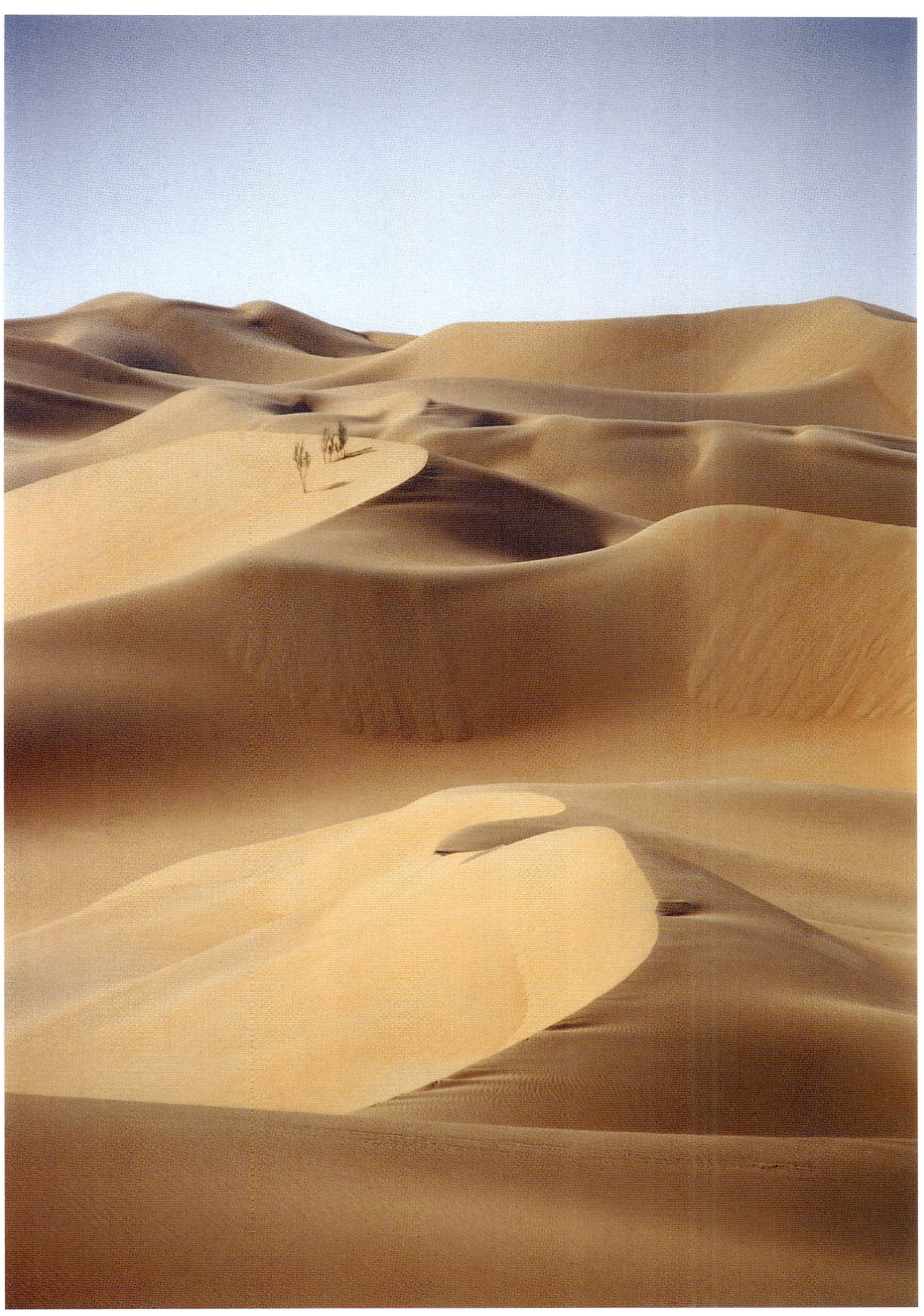

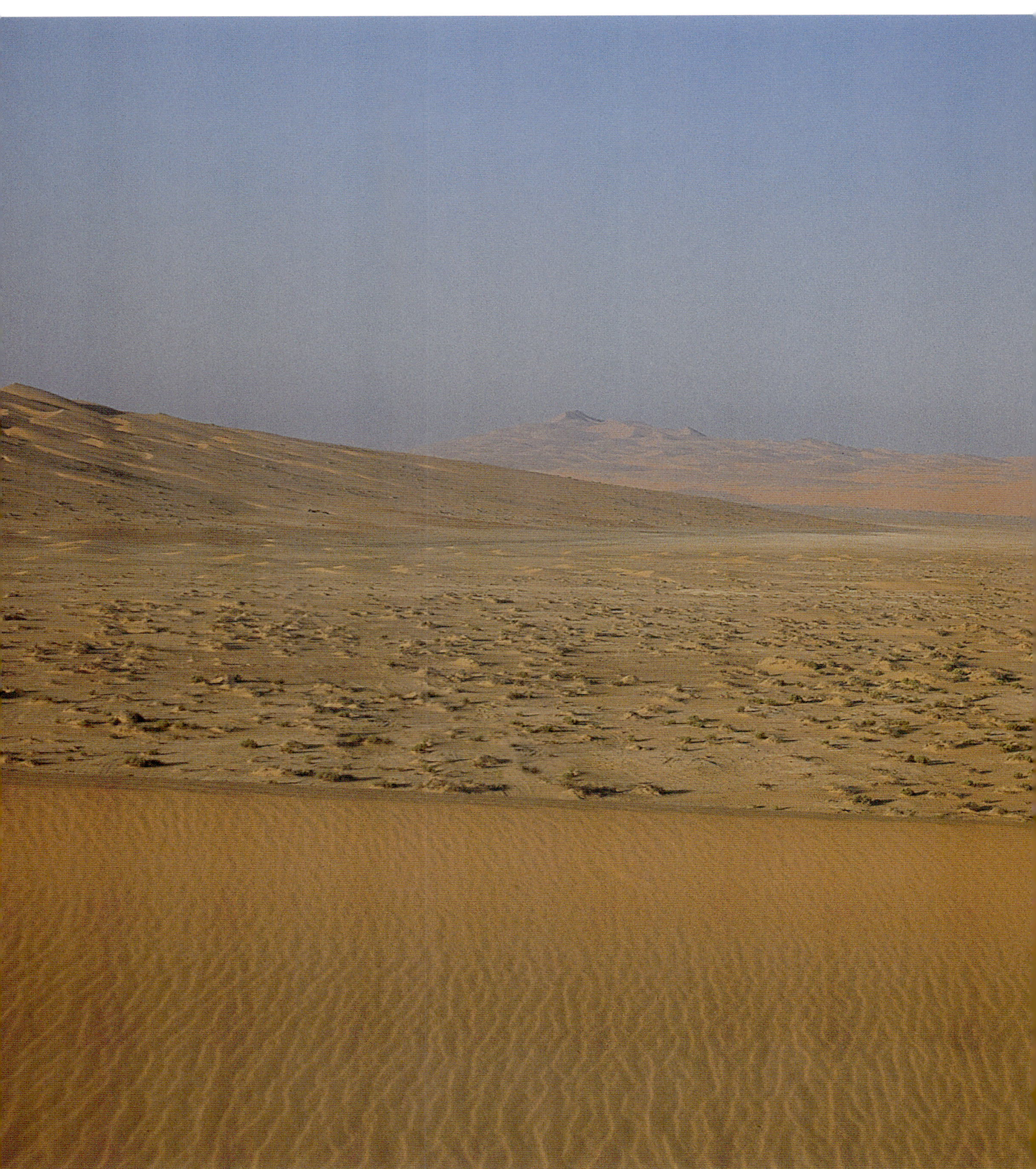

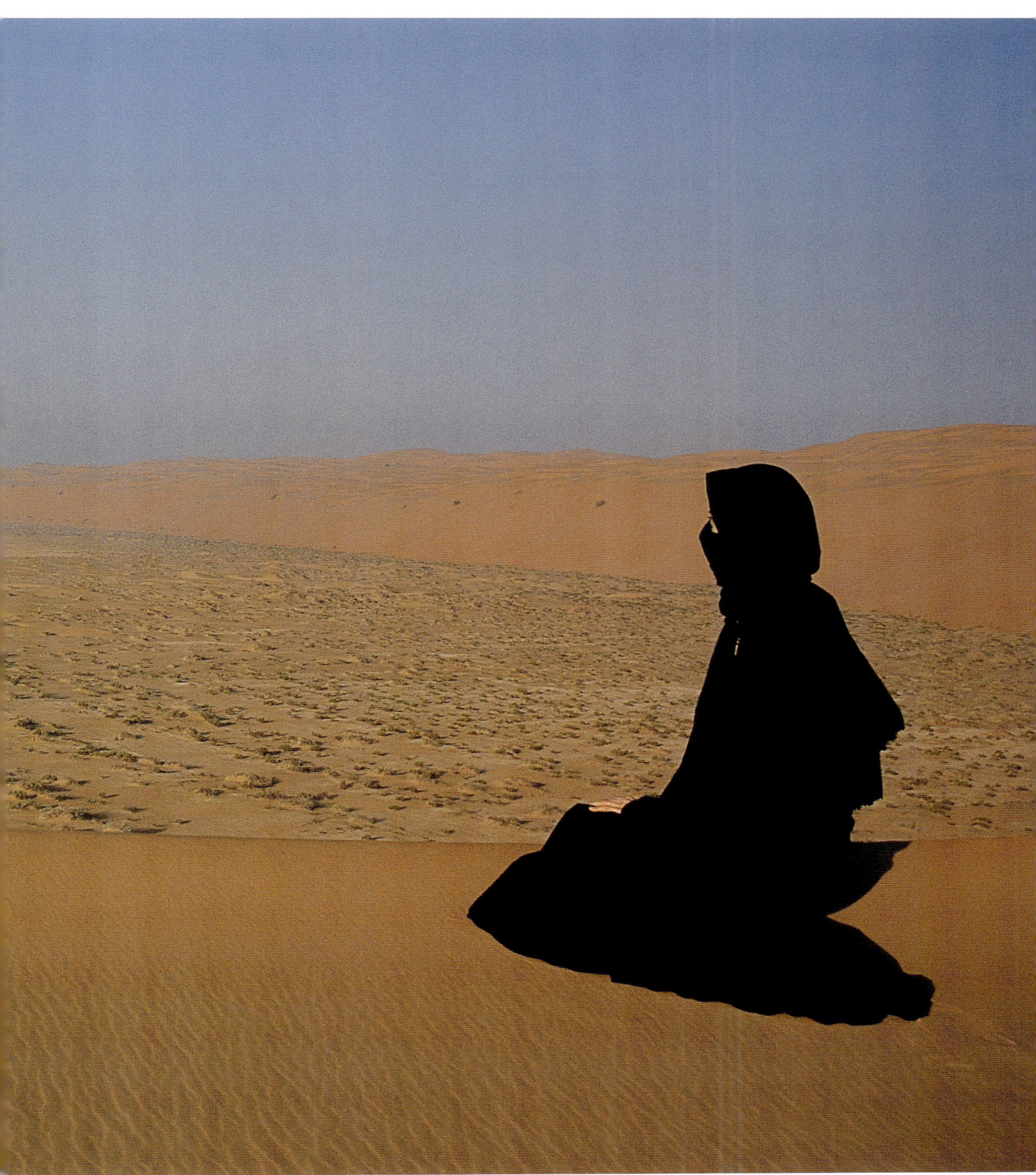

Lyrics of the Sands

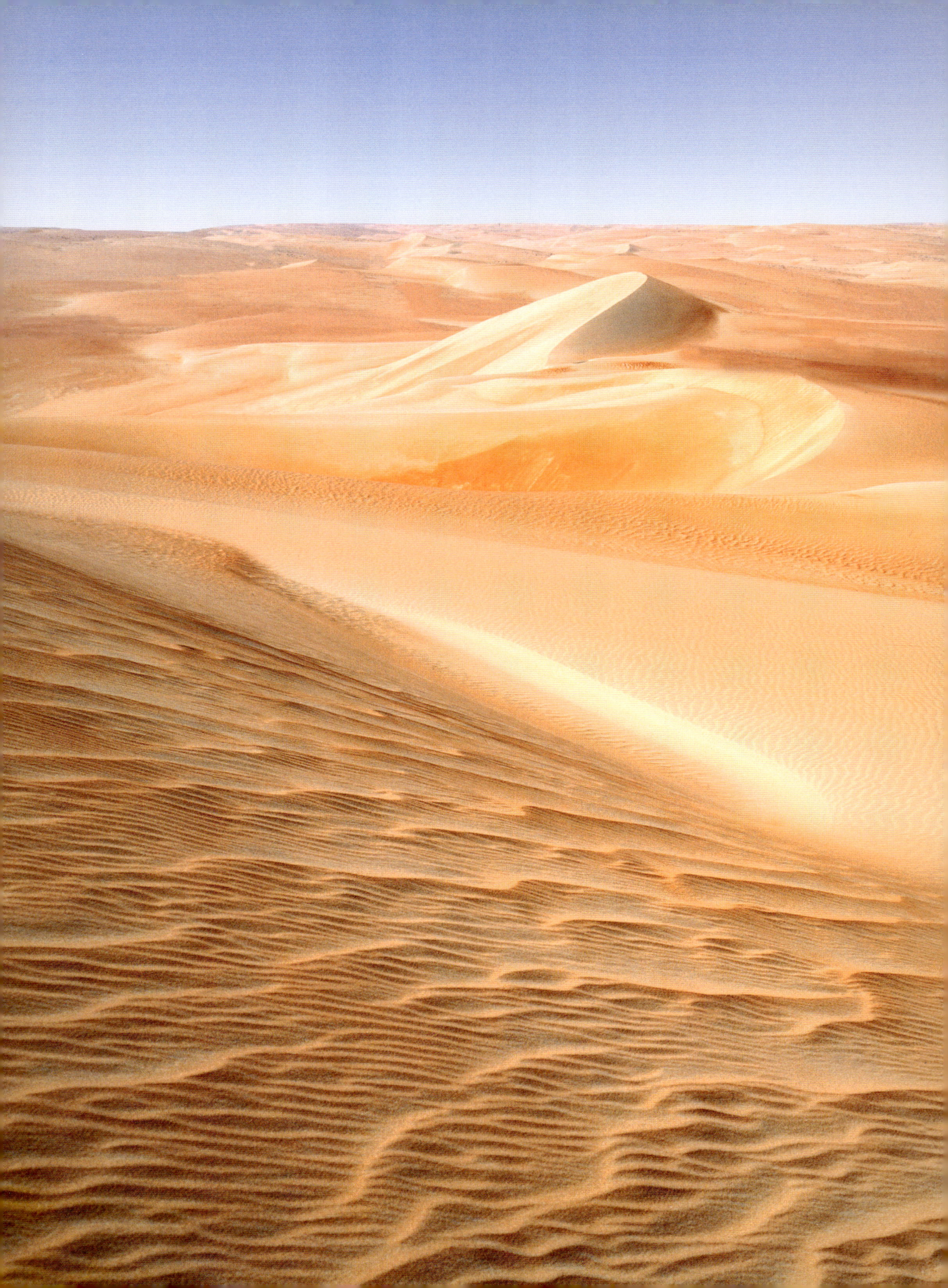

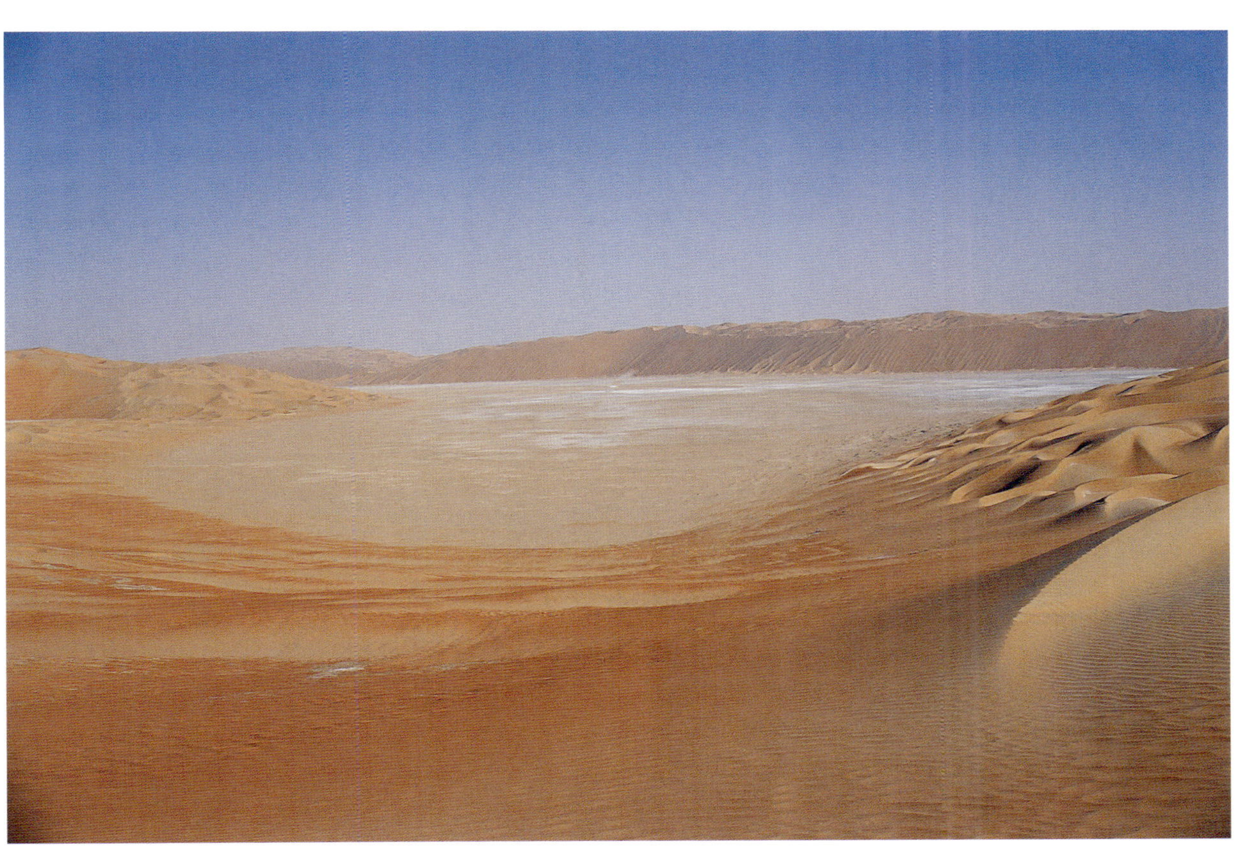

Lyrics of the Sands

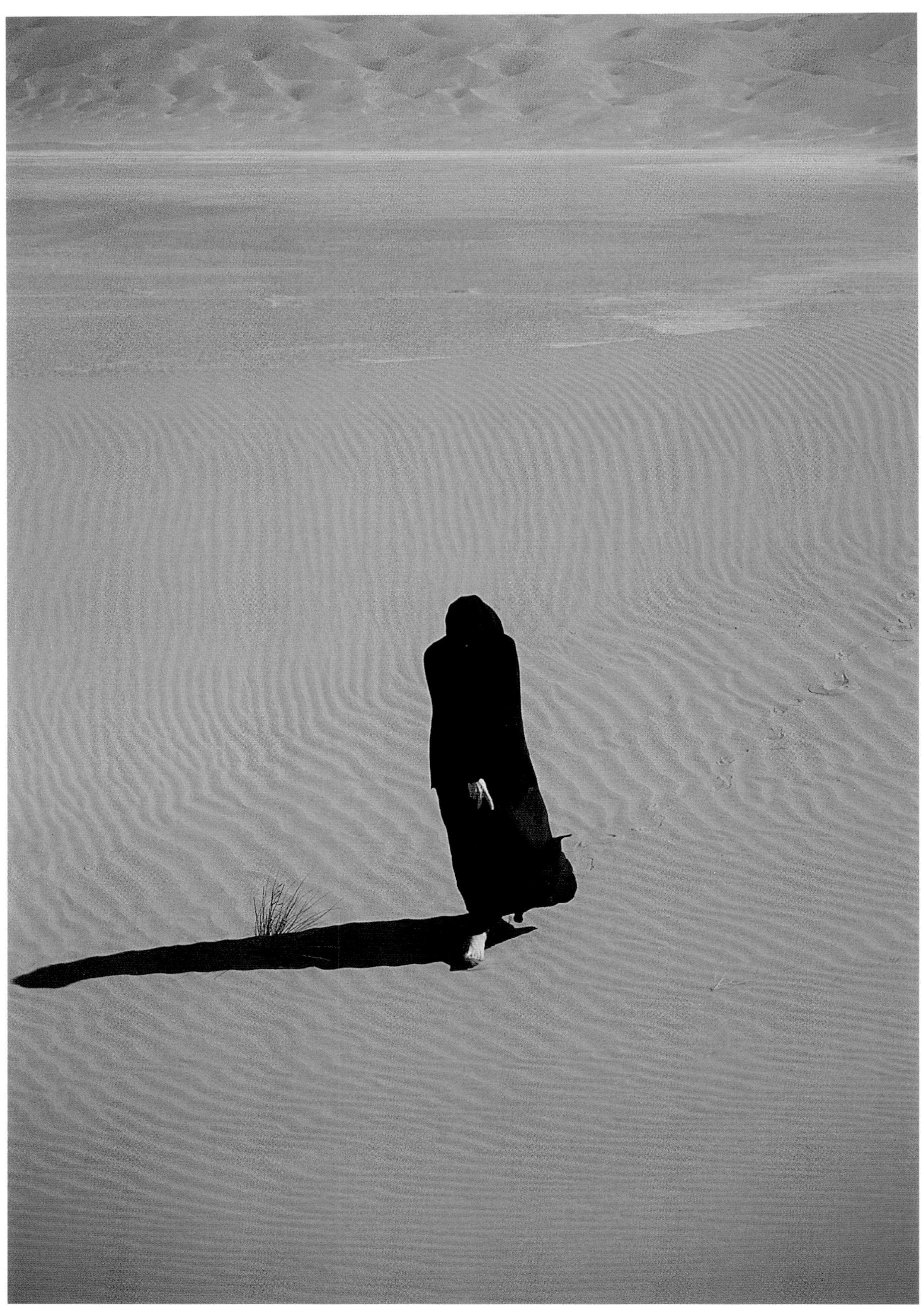

ذَرِينِي أَطُوفَ فِي البِلَادِ لَعَلَّنِي   أُخَلِّيكِ أَوْ أُغْنِيكِ عَنْ سُوءِ مَحْضَرِ

عُرْوَةَ بِن الوَرْد

Let me roam freely over the land, so that we may be free of the
evils of a settled life.

'Urwa bin al-Ward

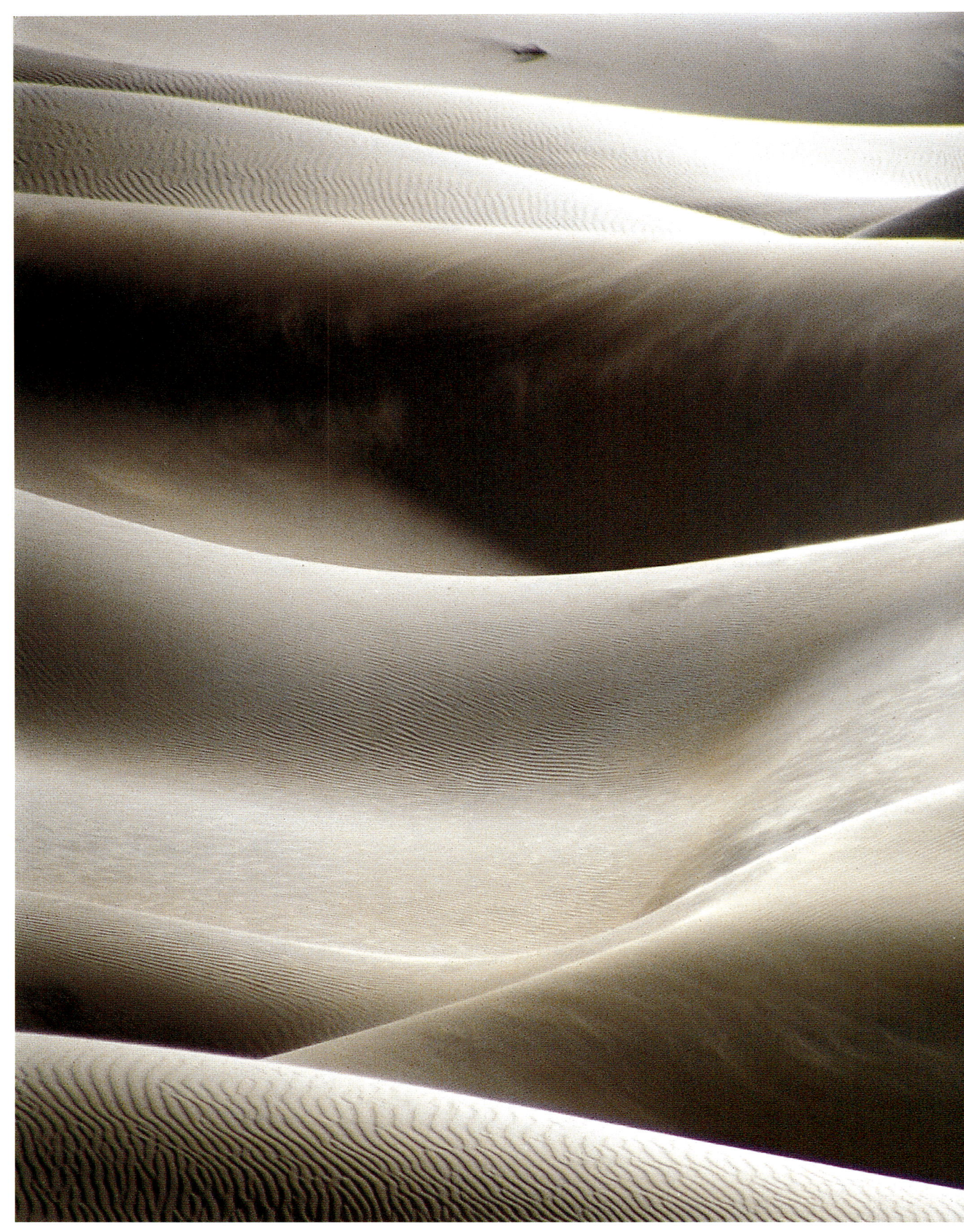

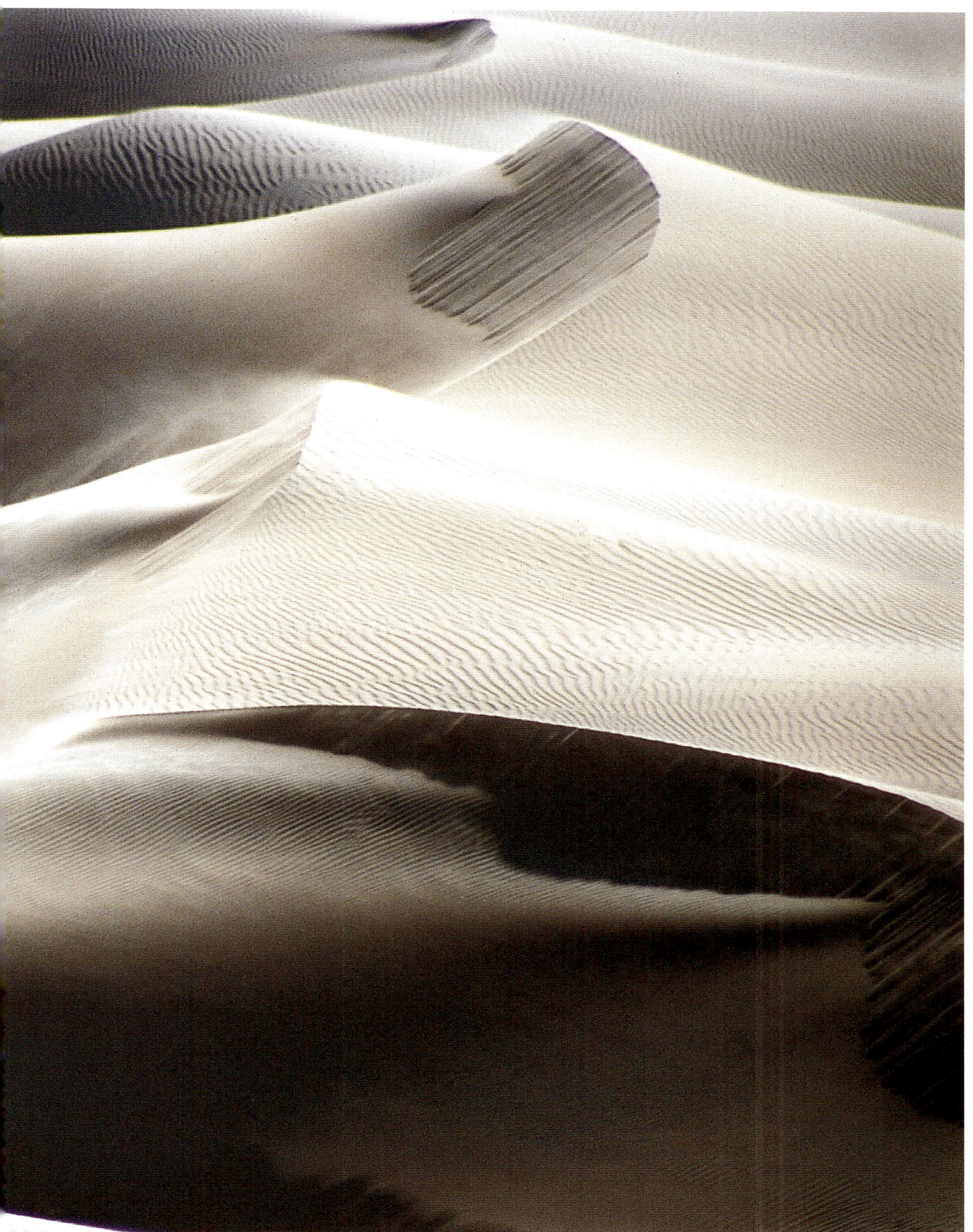

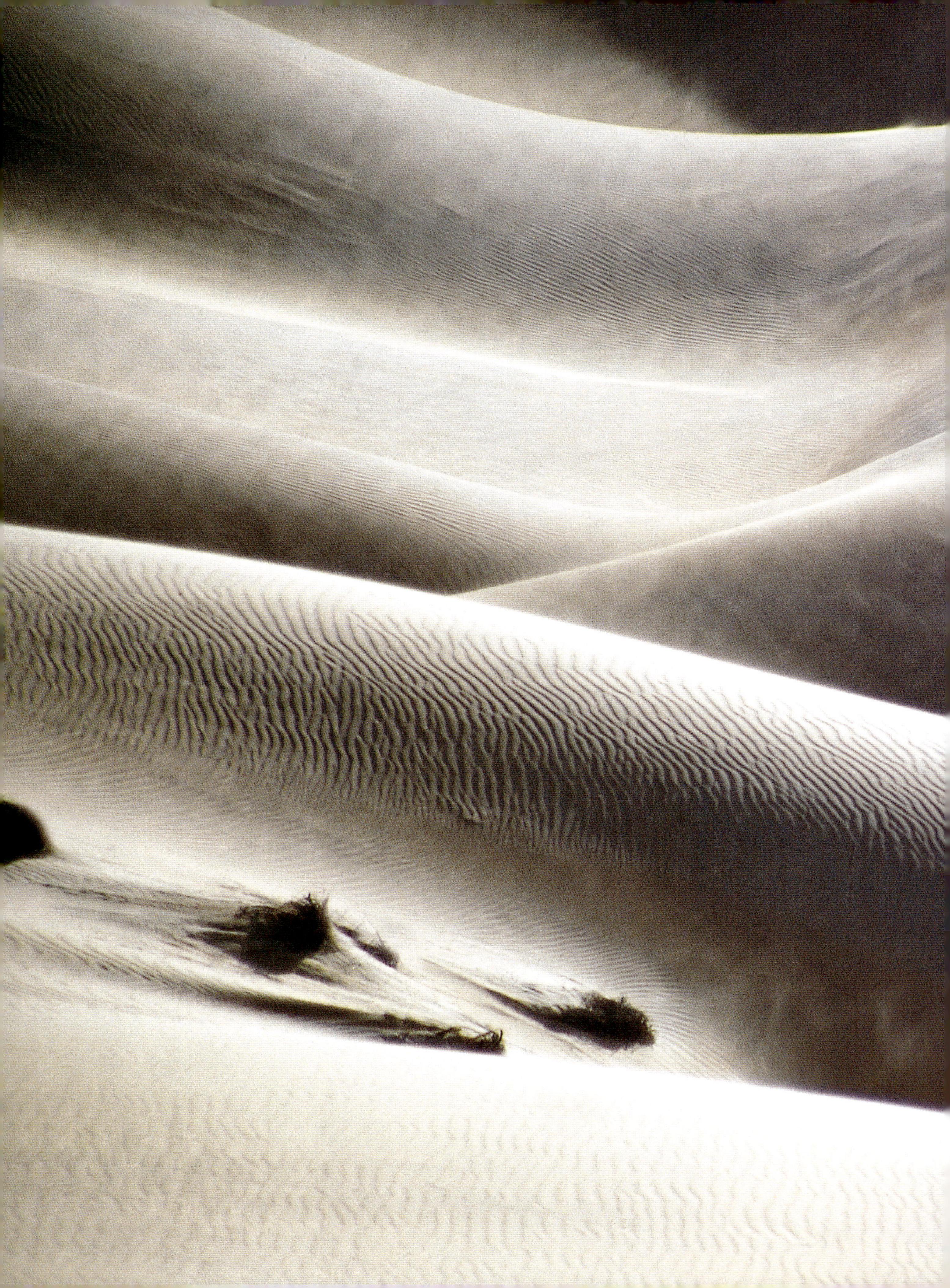

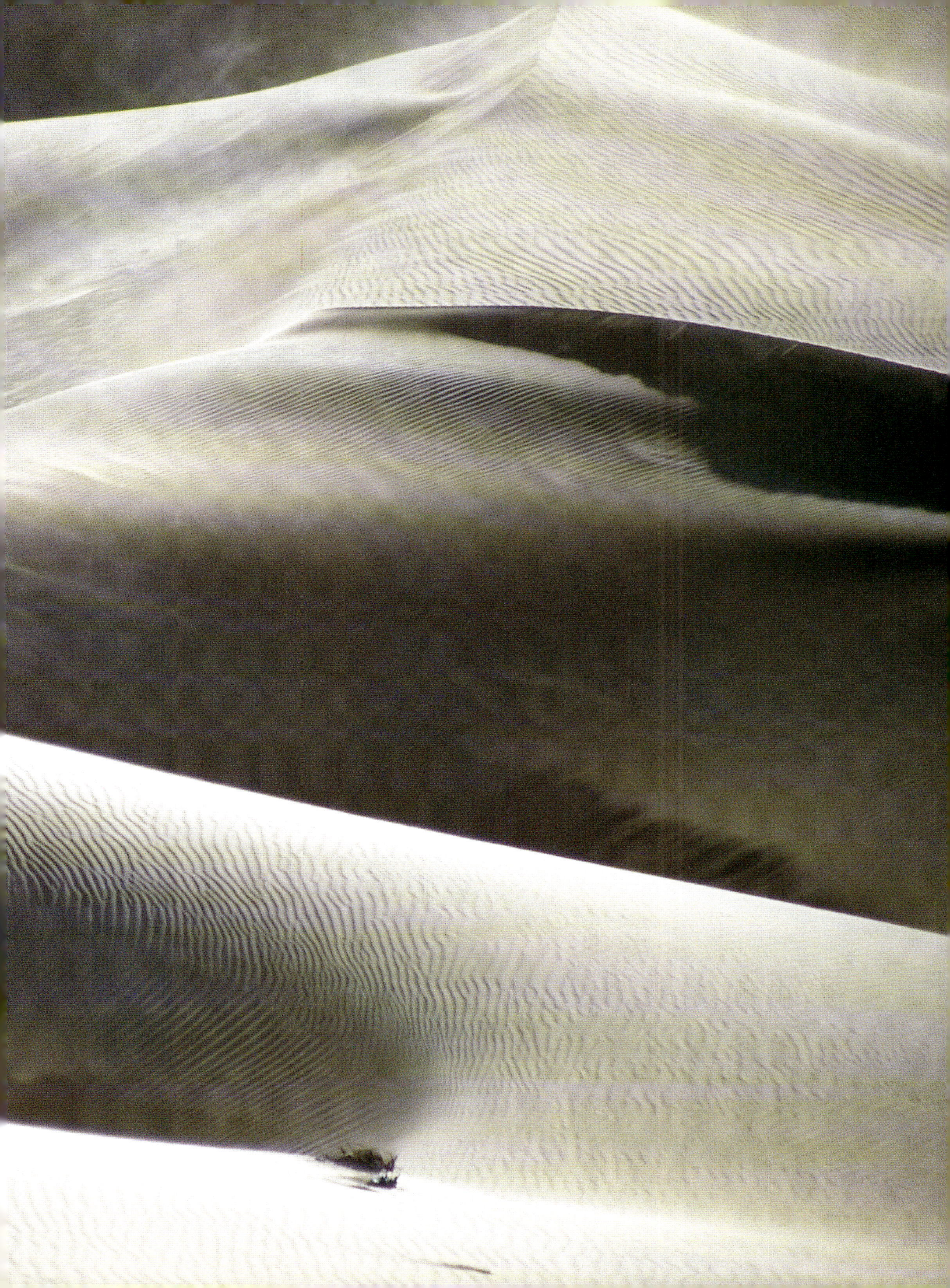

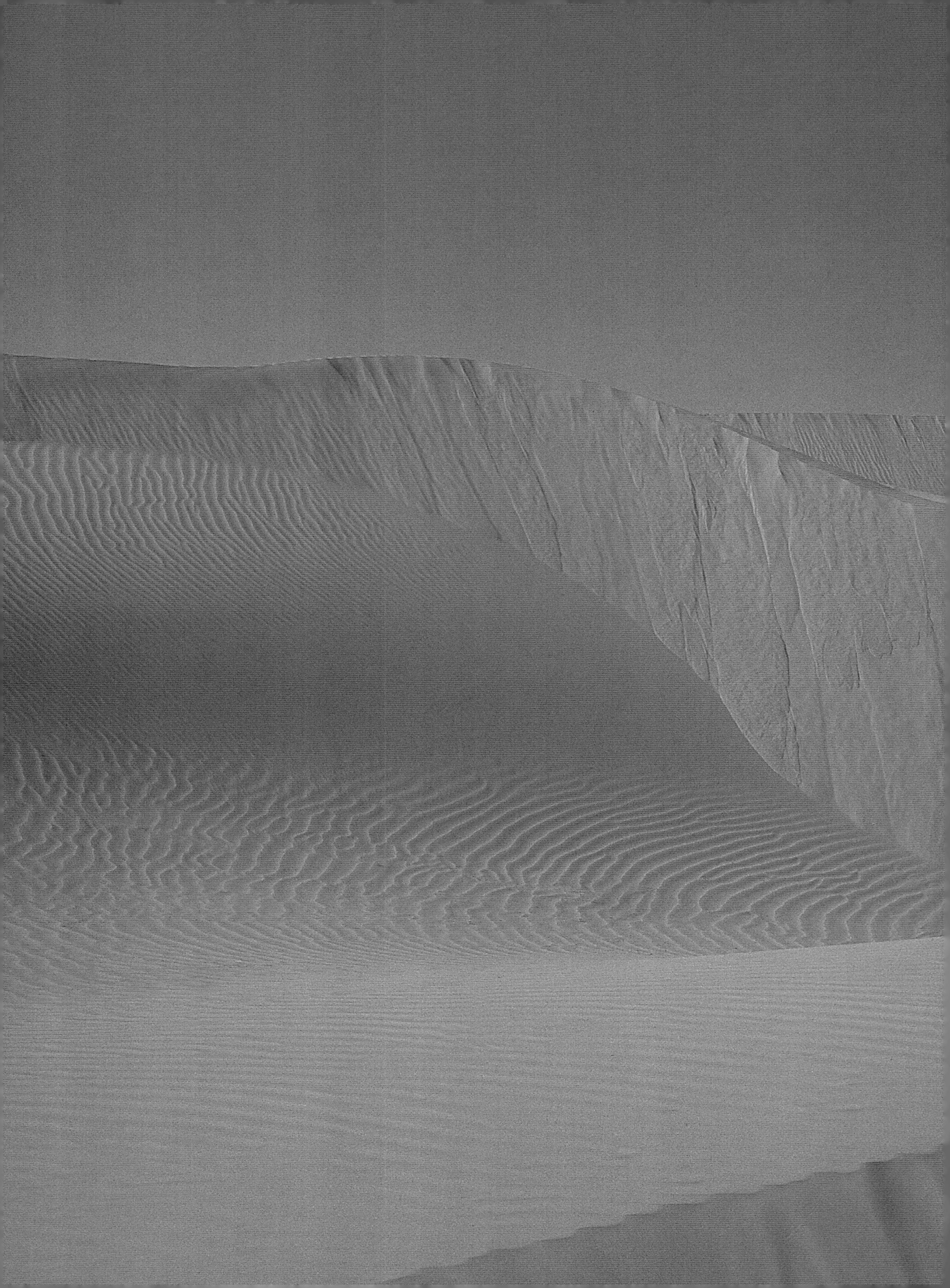

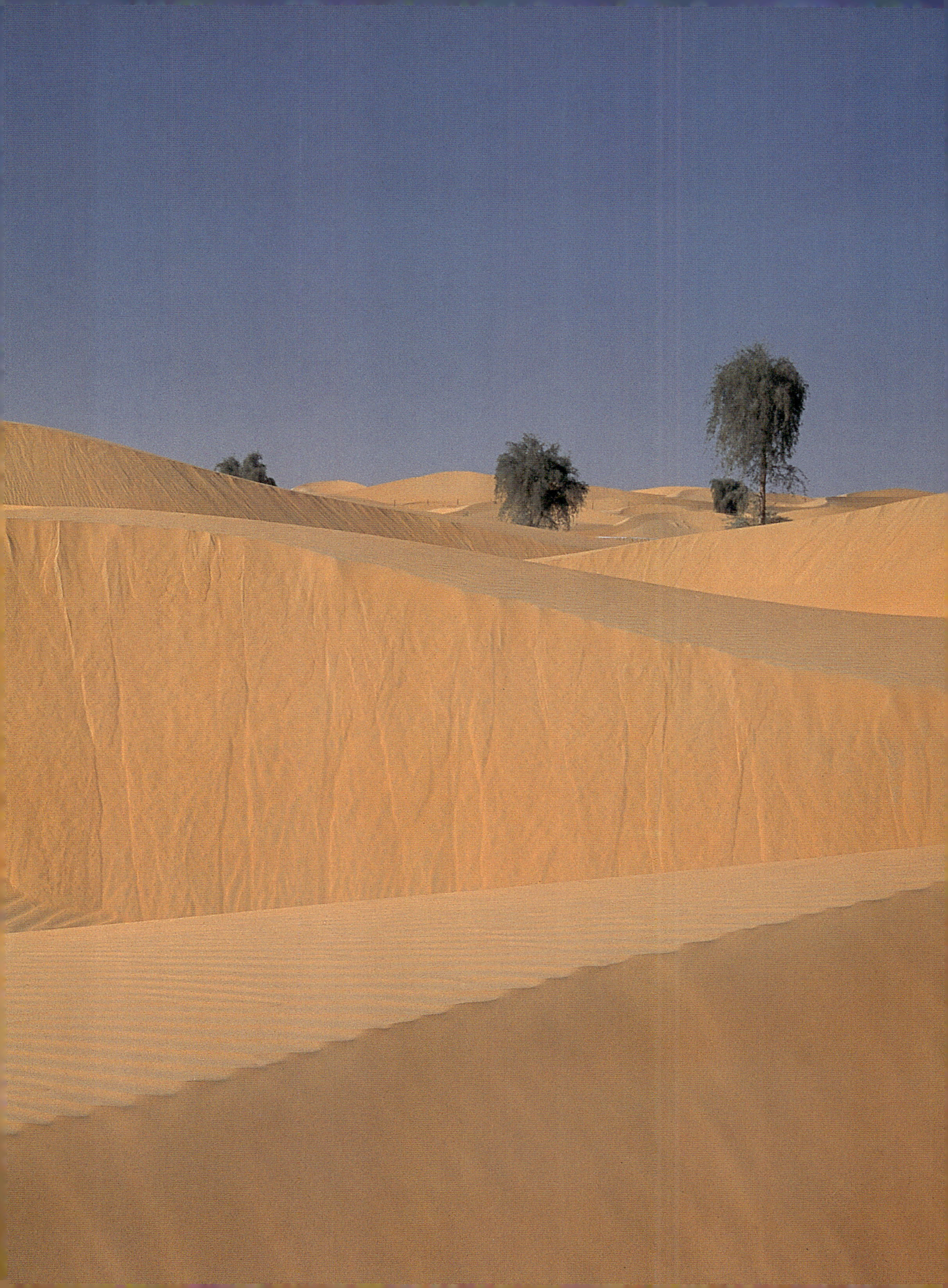

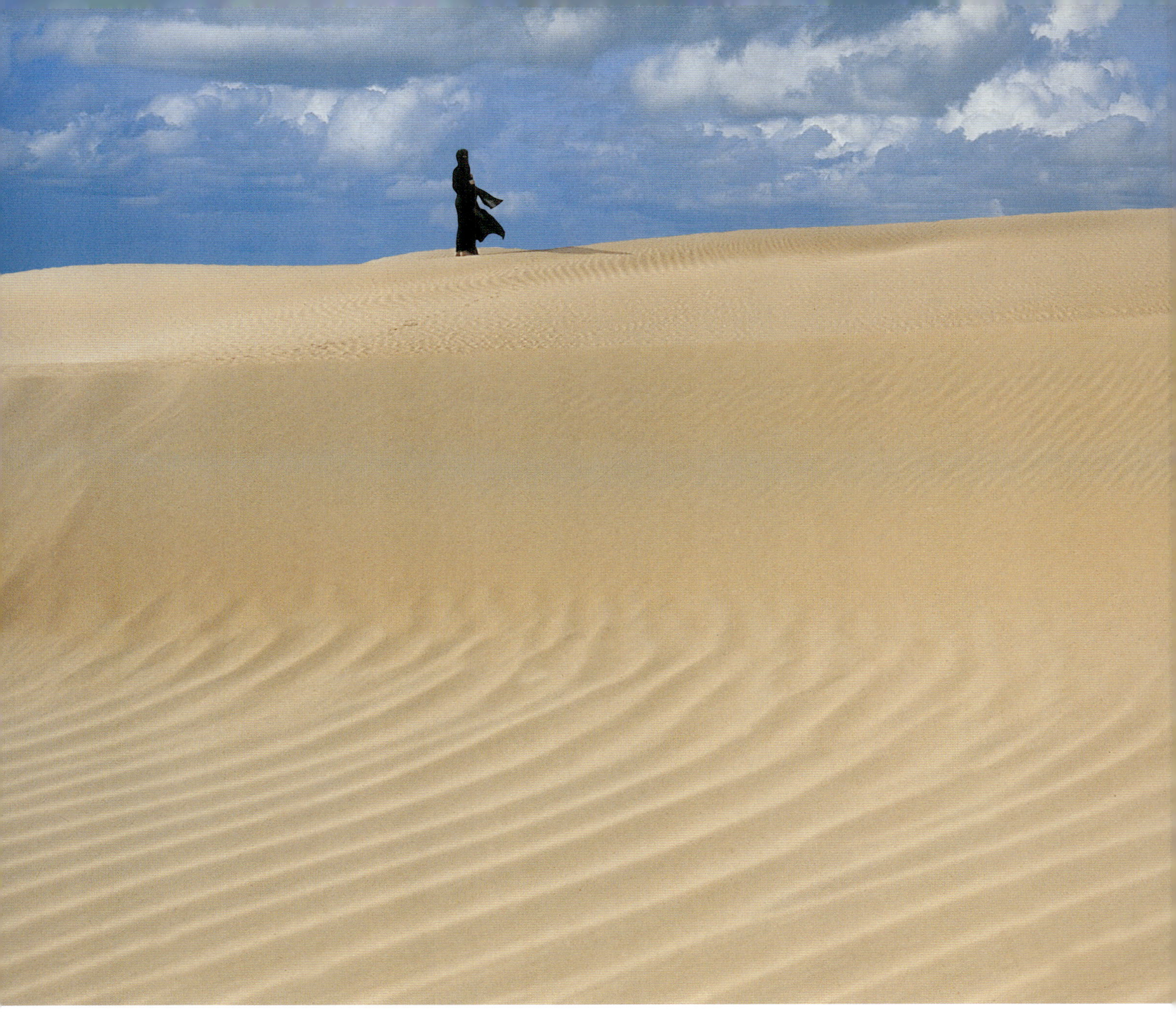

وَاسْتَفِّ تُرْبَ الأَرْضِ كَيْ لا يَرَى لَهُ   عَلَيَّ مِنَ الطَّوْلِ امْرُؤٌ مُتَطَوِّلُ

وَلَوْلا اجْتِنَابُ الذَّأْمِ لَمْ يُلْفَ مَشْرَبٌ   يُعَاشُ بِهِ إِلّا لَدَيَّ وَمَأْكَلُ

الشَّنْفَرَى الأَزْدِي

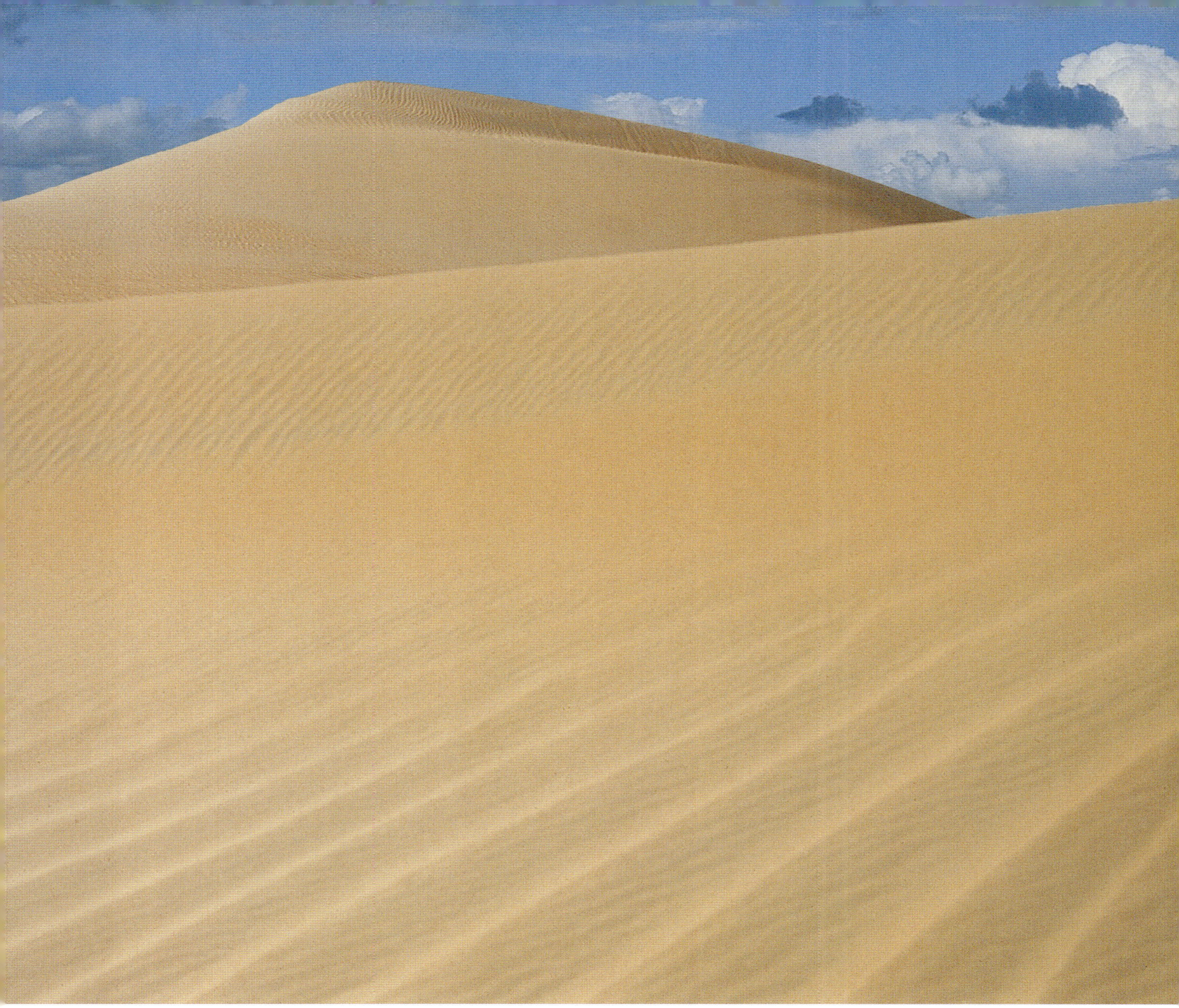

And I would lick the dry dust of the earth rather than
allow a boastful man to think that I owe him generosity.

Were it not for the risk of shame, there is nothing which sustains life
that I could not have had.

Al-Shanfara al-Azdi

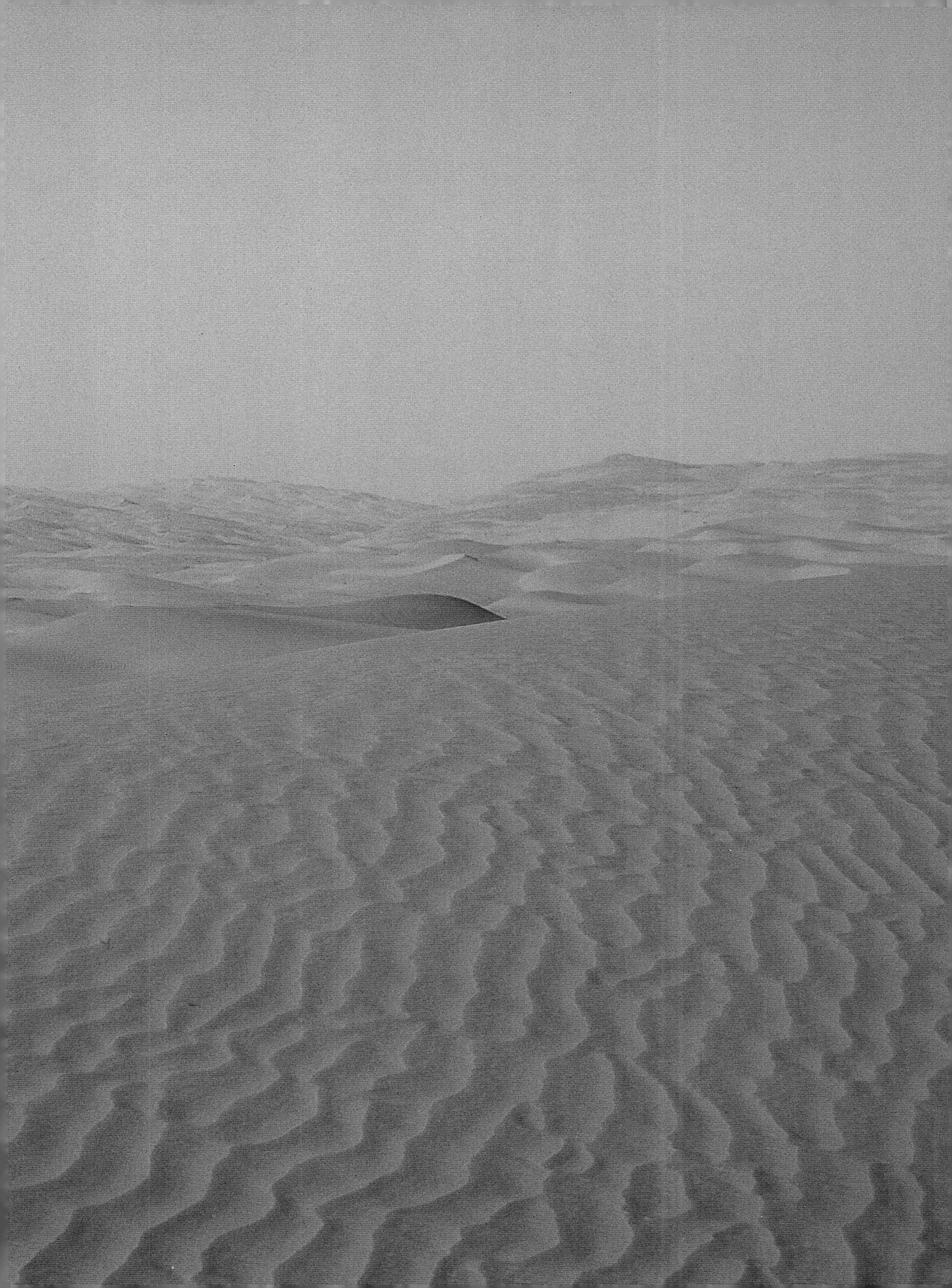

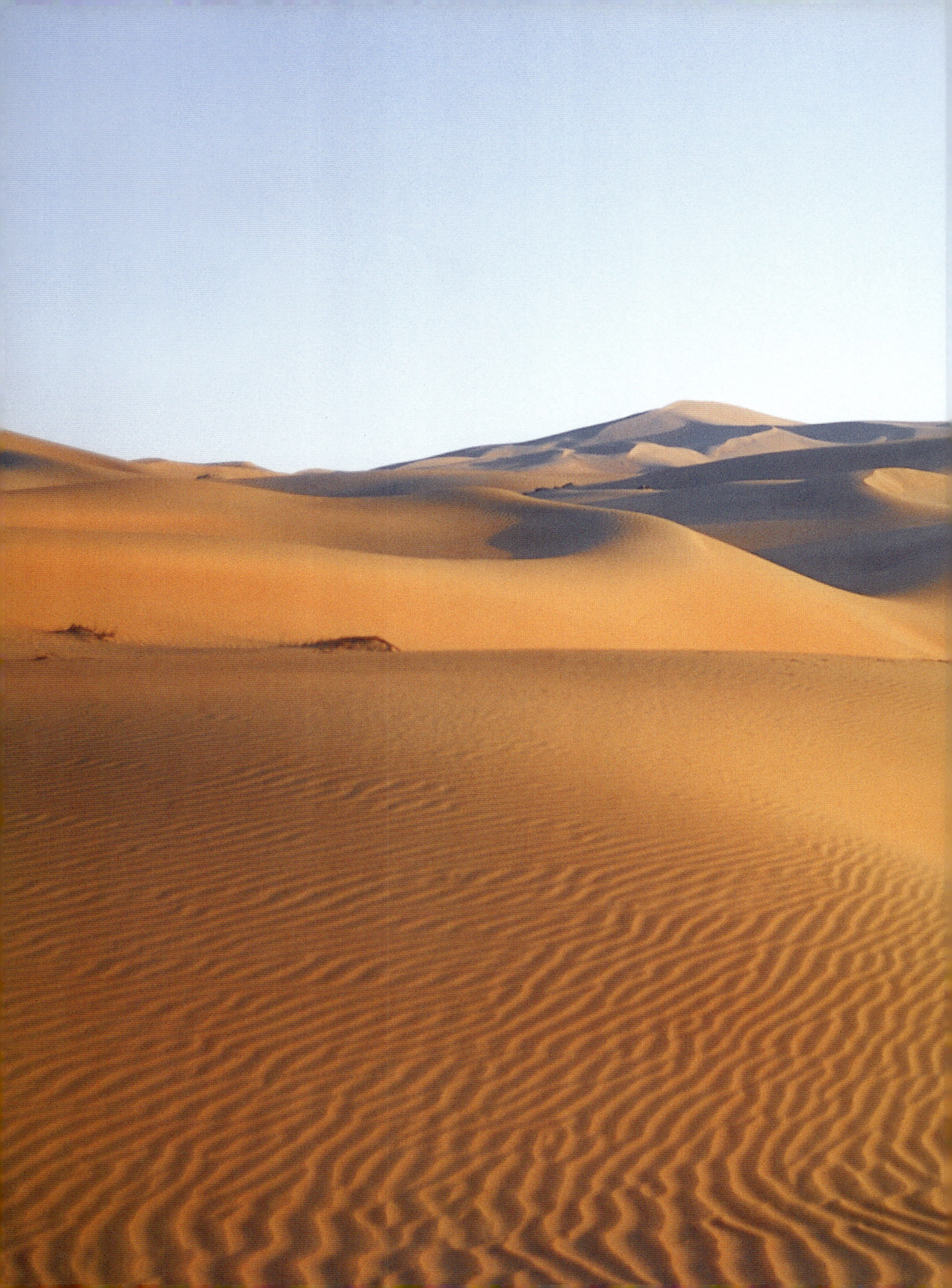

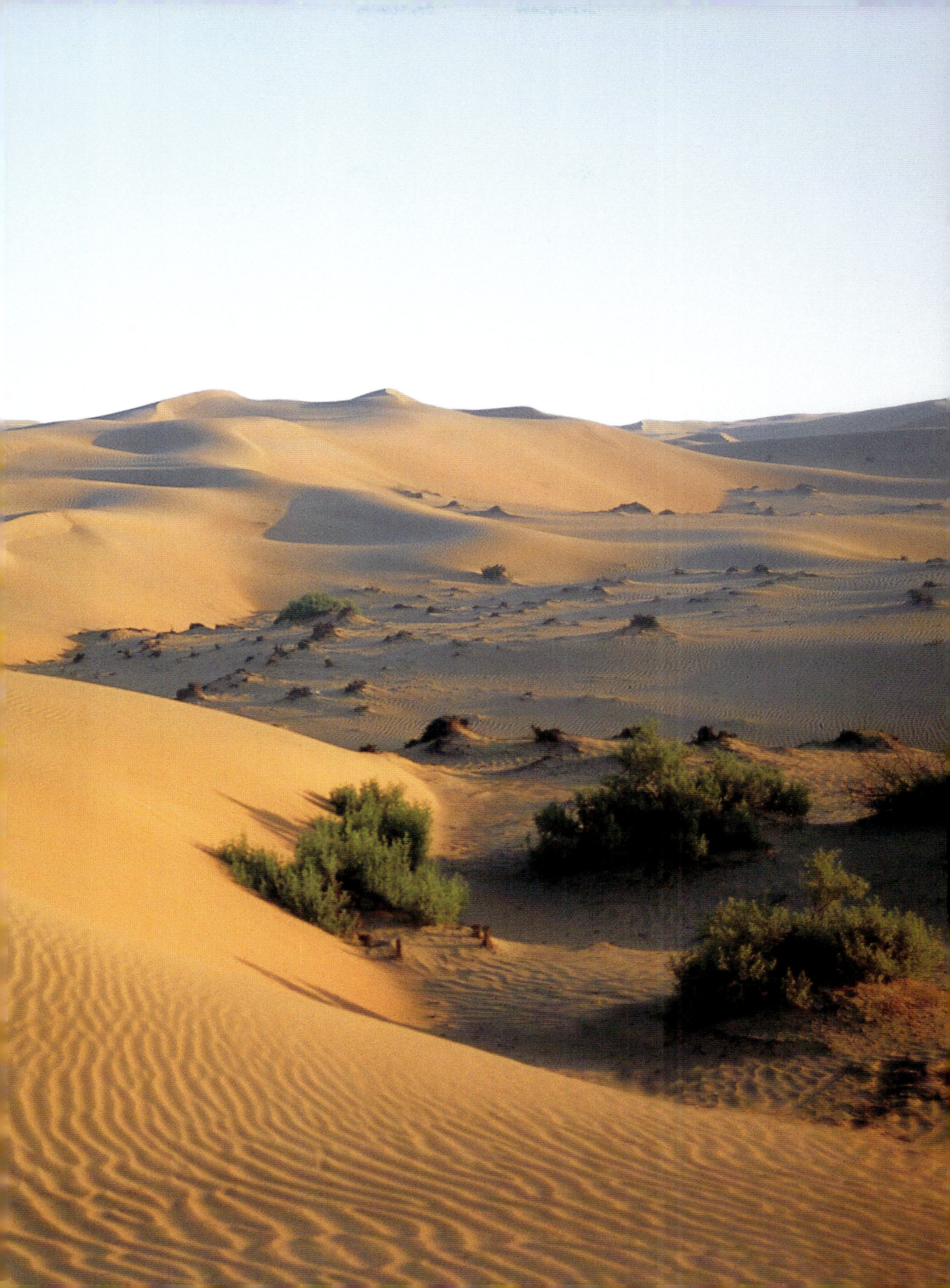

وَأَغْدُو عَلَى القُوتِ الزَّهِيدِ كَمَا غَدَا   أَزَلُّ   تَهَادَاهُ   التَّنَائِفُ   أَطْحَلُ

الشَّنْفَرَى الأَزْدِي

I spend my mornings on scanty sustenance, like the agile, ash-grey wolf,
in the barren stretches of desert which lead from one to another.

Al-Shanfara al-Azdi

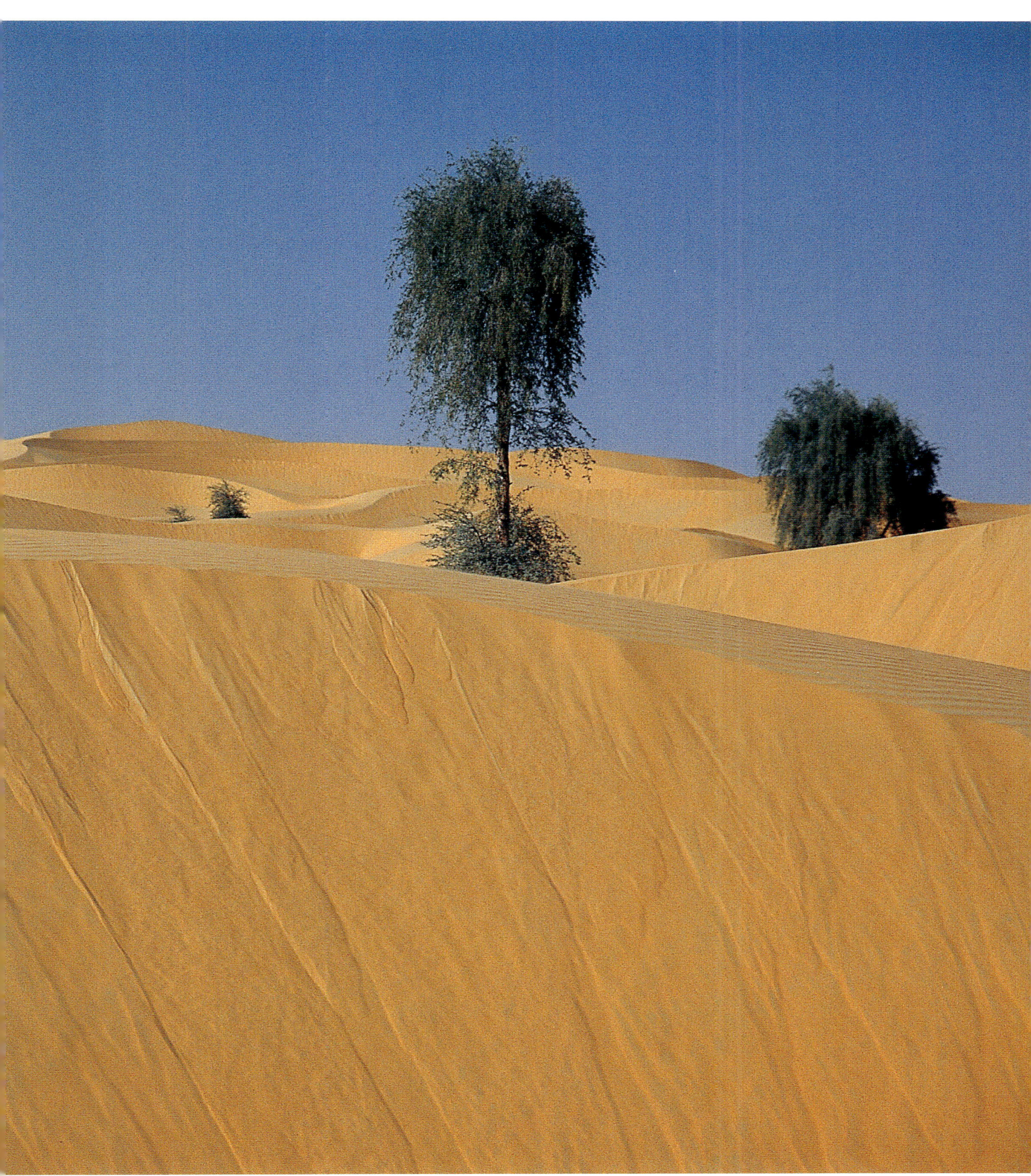

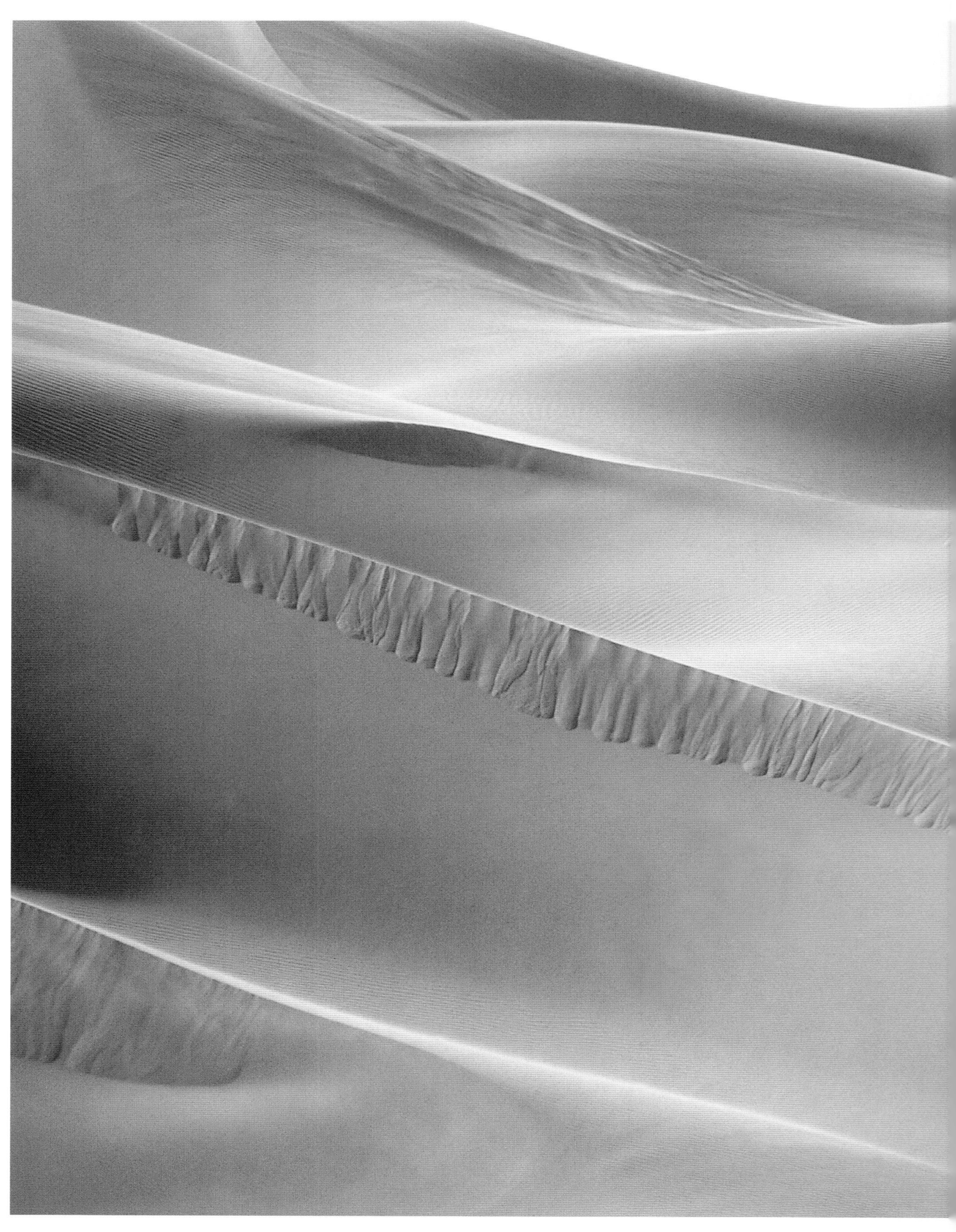

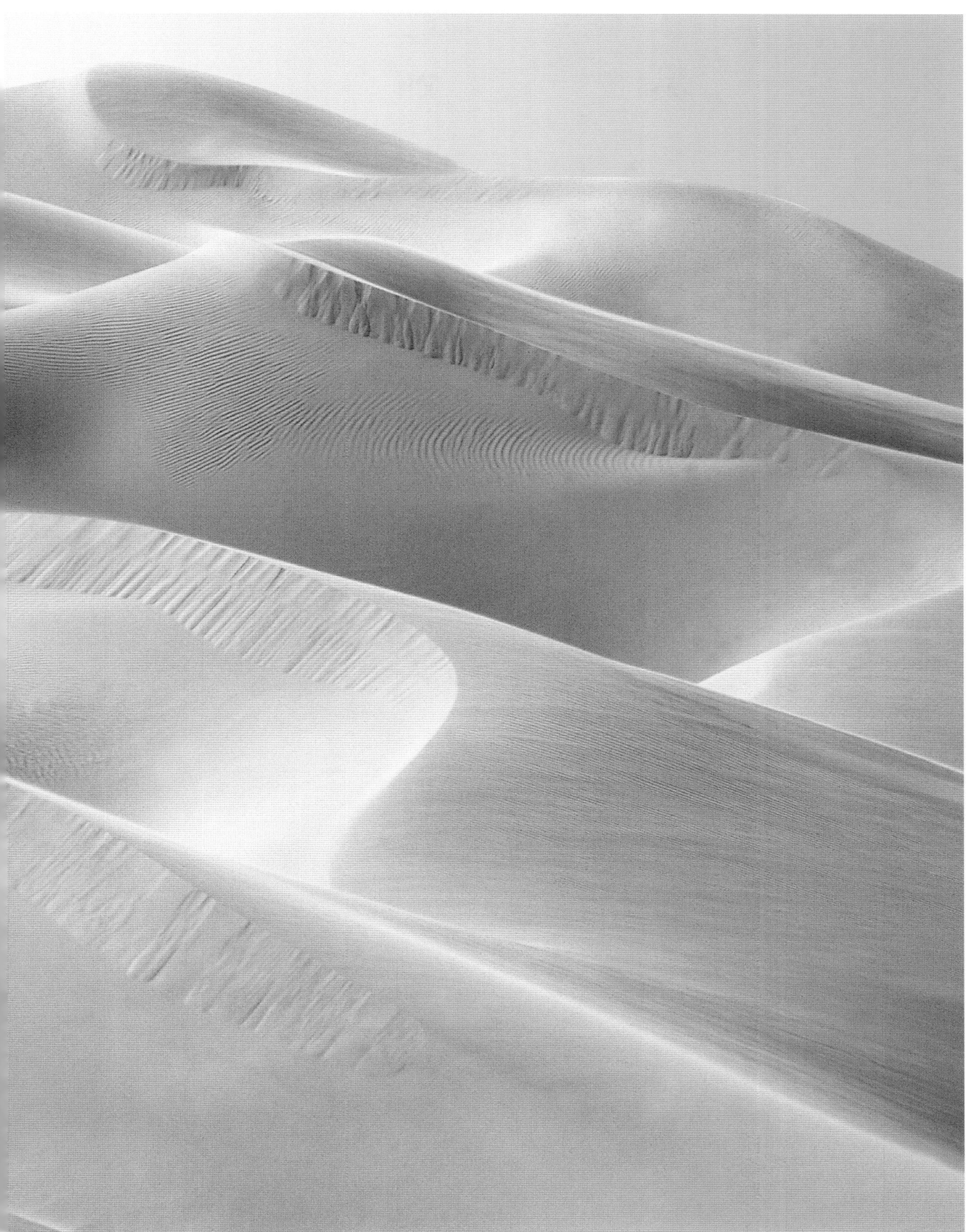

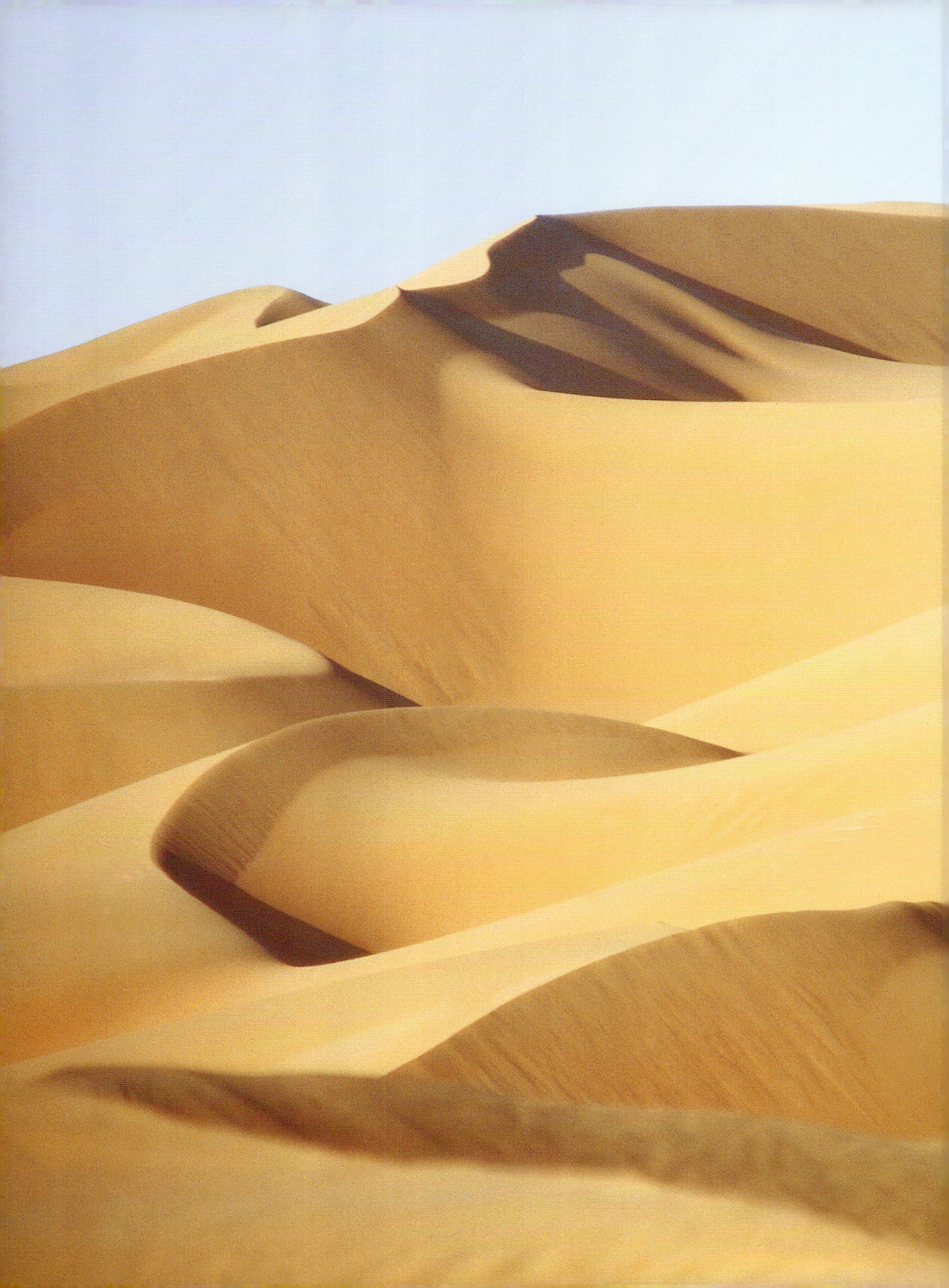

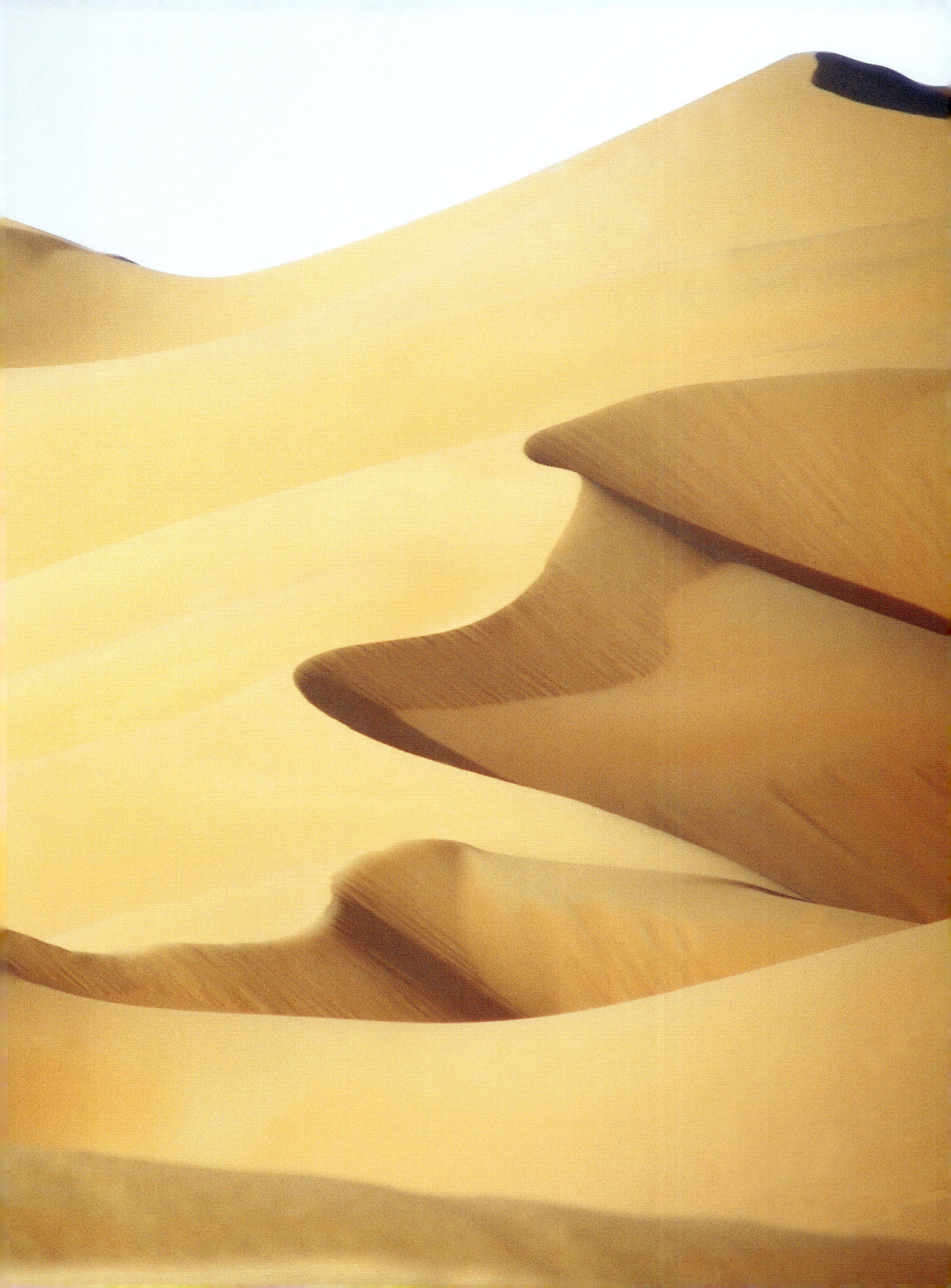

وَخَرْقٍ تَجَاوَزْتَ مَجْهُولَهُ   بِوَجْنَاءَ حَرْفٍ تَشَكَّى الكَلالَا

فَكُنْتَ النَّهَارَ بِهِ شَمْسَهُ   وَكُنْتَ اللَّيْلِ فِيهِ هِلالَا

جَنُوب الهُذَلِيَّة

Many a desert, wind-swept and unknown, have you crossed
on a strong she-camel, lean and swift, yet complaining of fatigue.

By day you were the desert's sun, and in the darkness of the night
you were a crescent moon shining upon it.

Janub Al-Huðhaliyyah

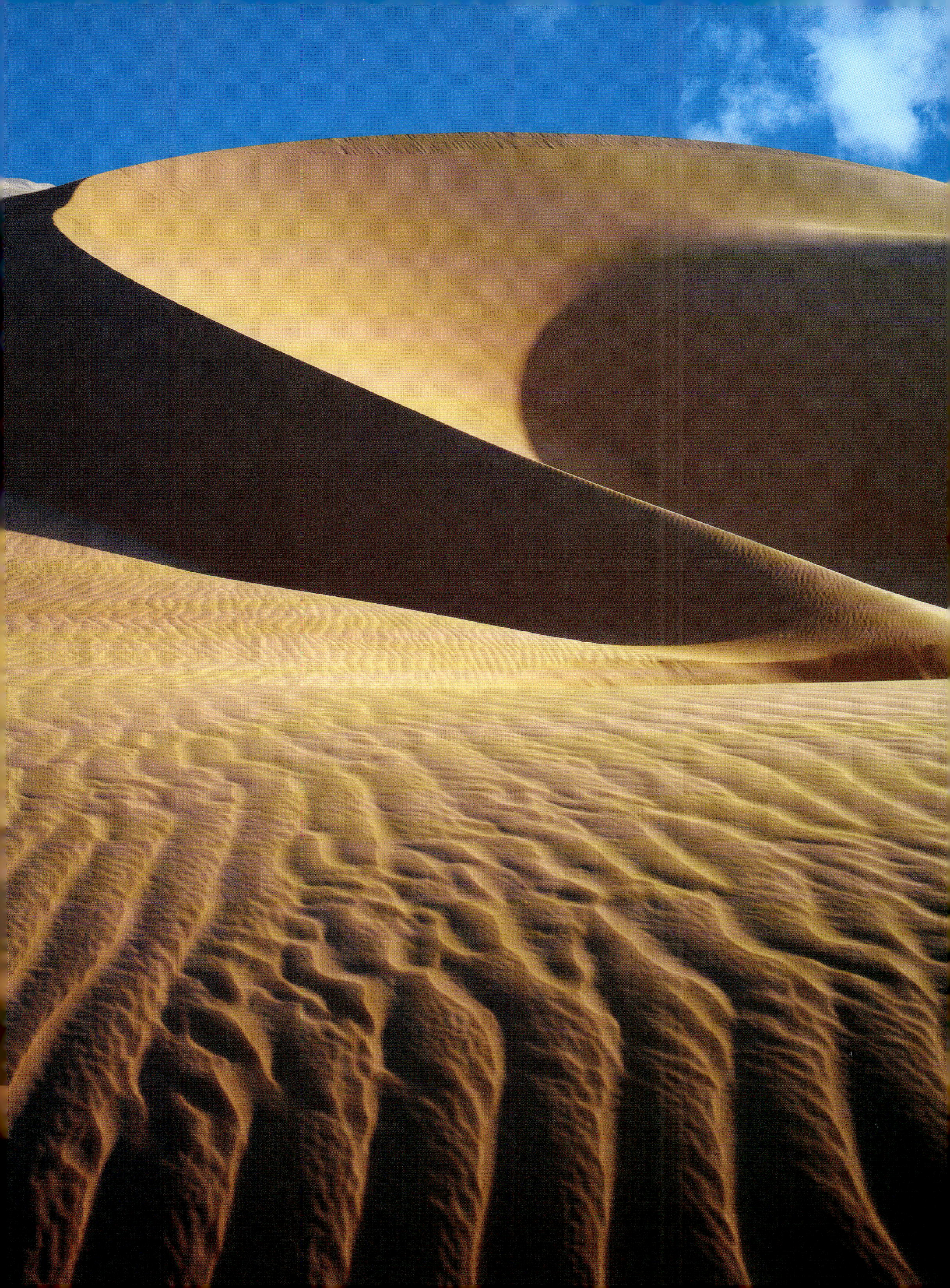

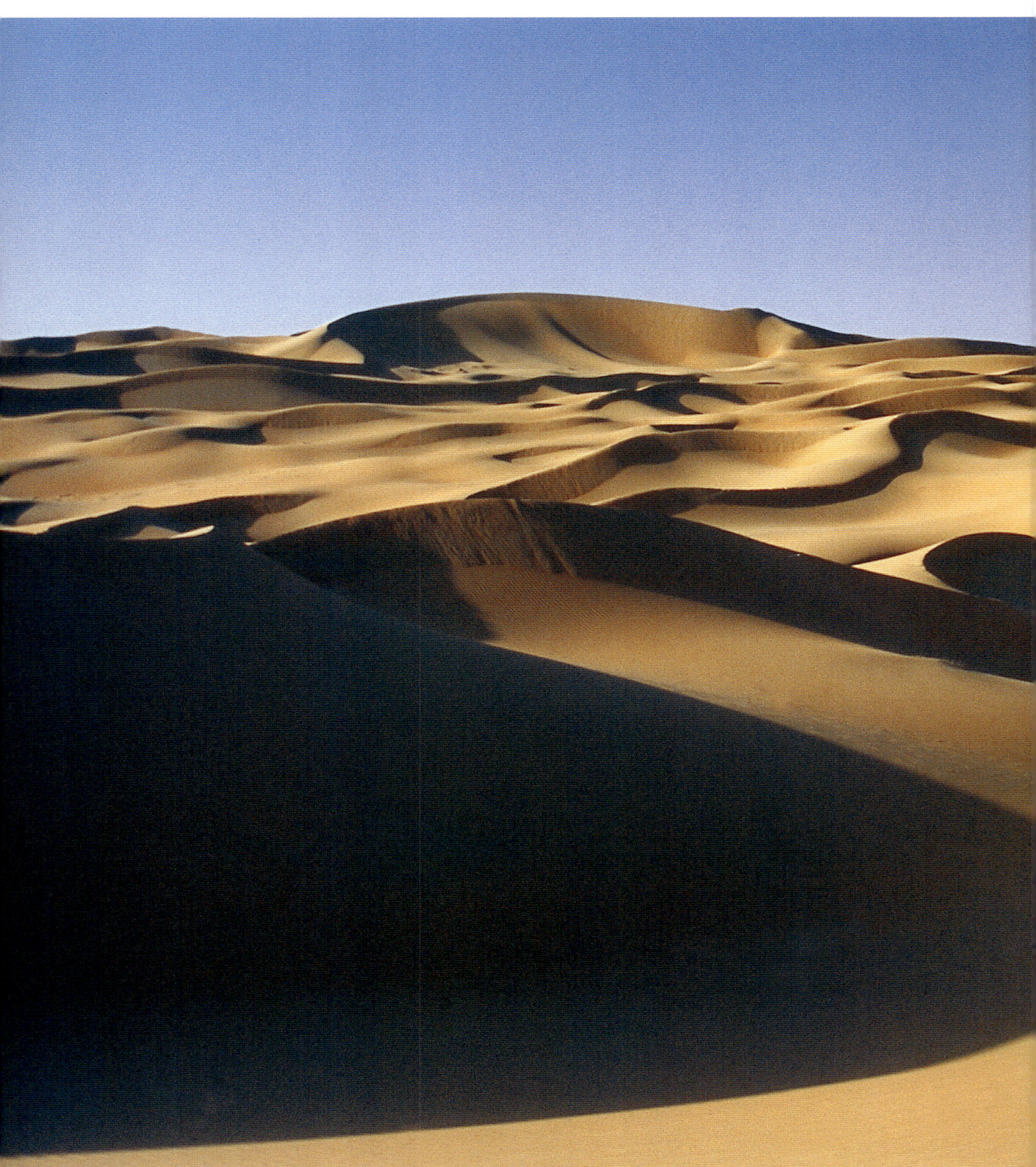

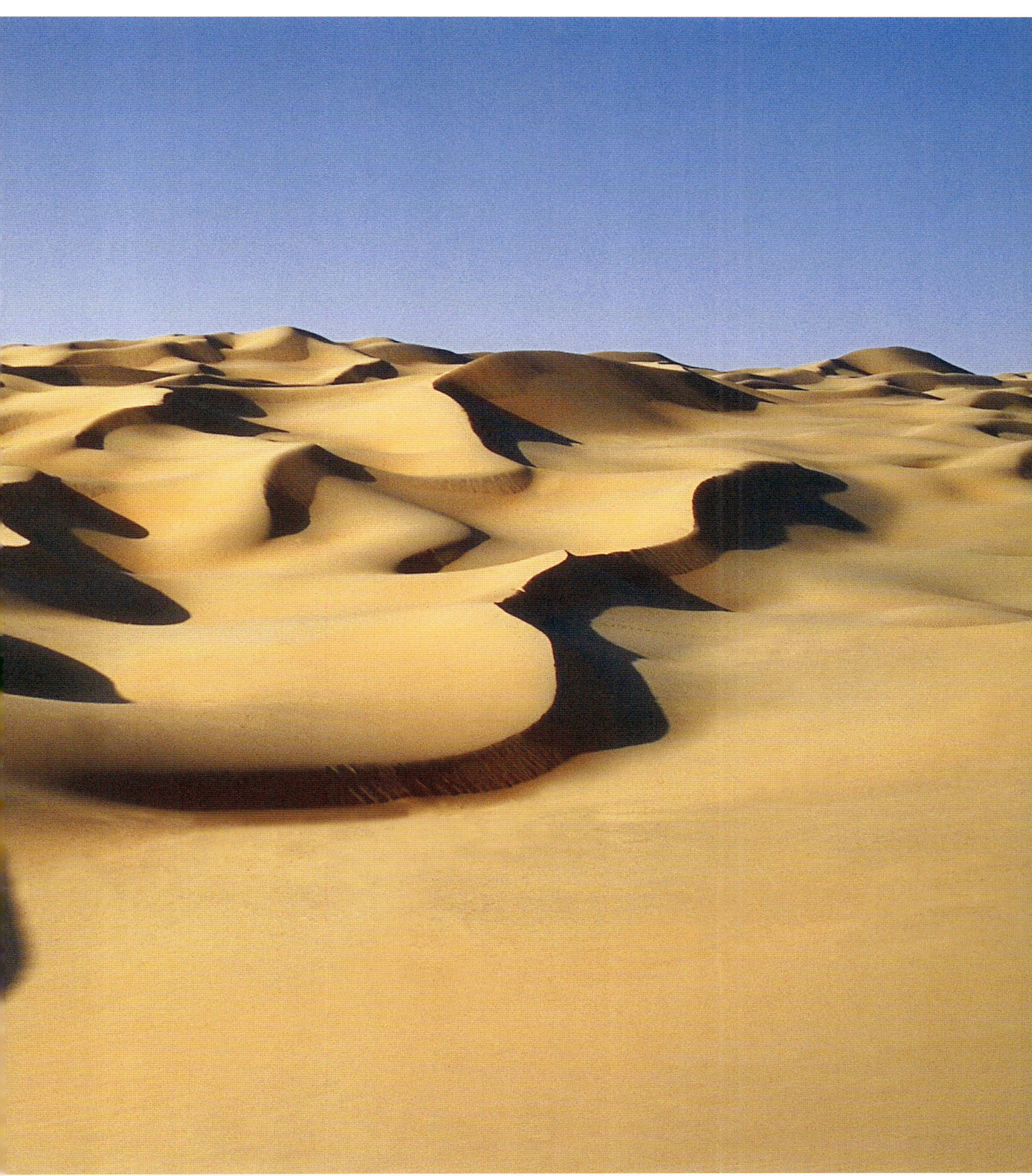

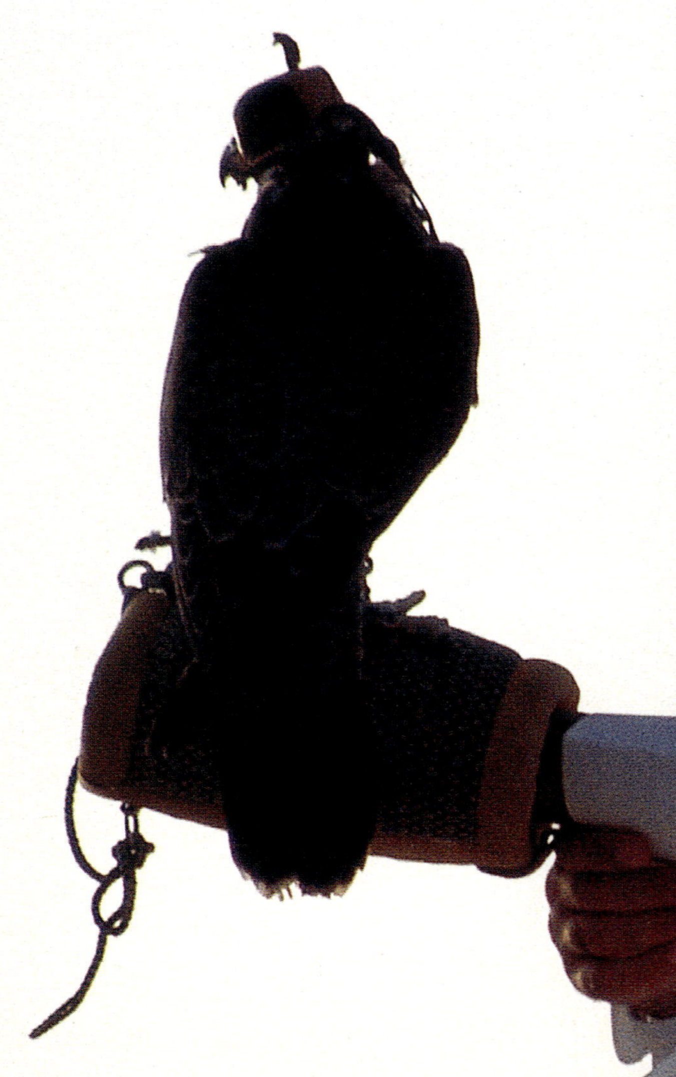

وَمَا النَّاسُ إِلّا كَالدِّيَارِ وَأَهْلُهَا   بِهَا يَوْمَ حَلُّوهَا وَغَدَوْا بَلَاقِعُ

لَبِيد بِنْ رَبِيعَةَ العَامِرِي

Men are like desert encampments,
dwellers only for the day,
and next morning they are gone.

Labid bin Rabiyya'a al-Amiri

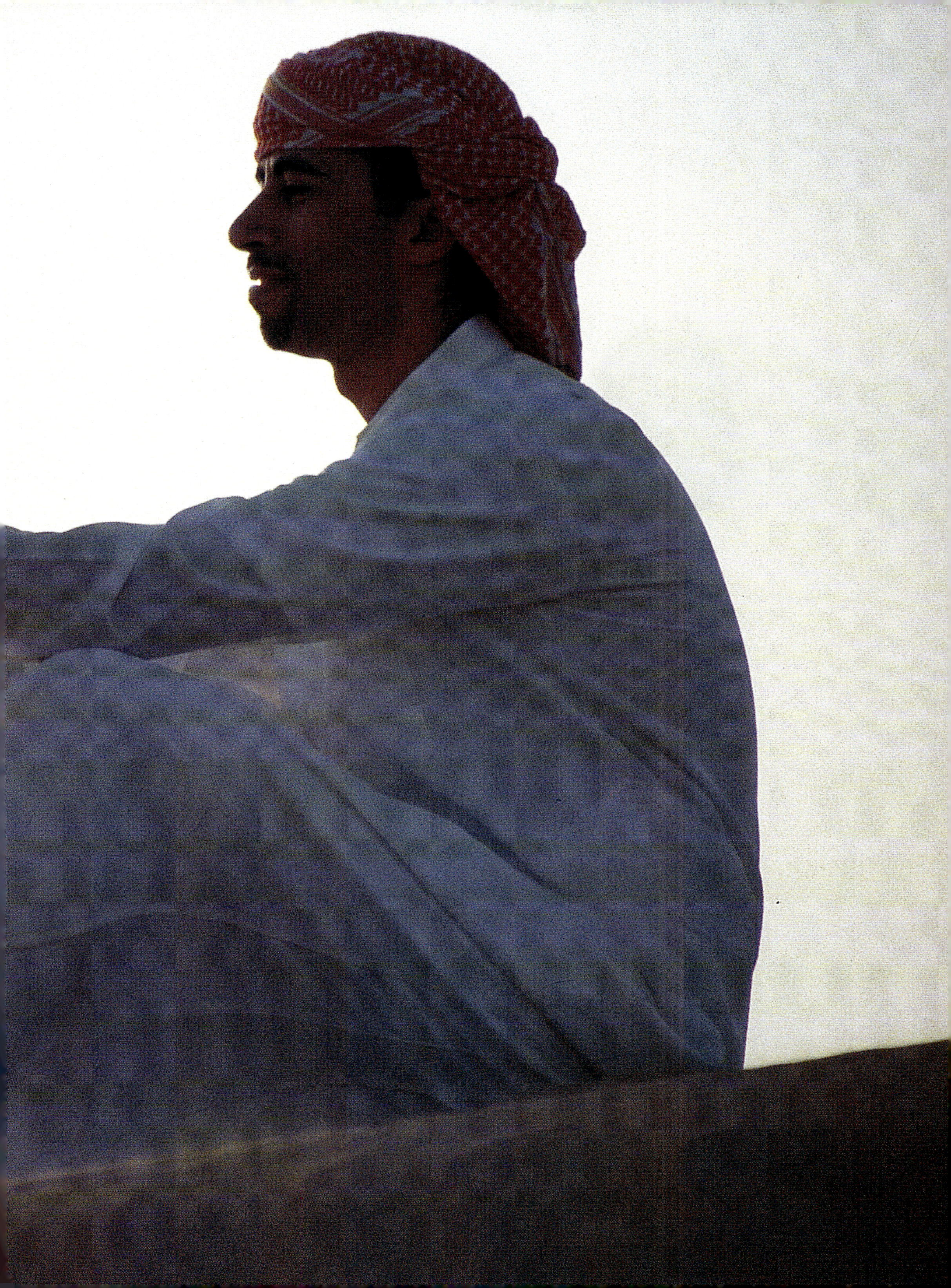

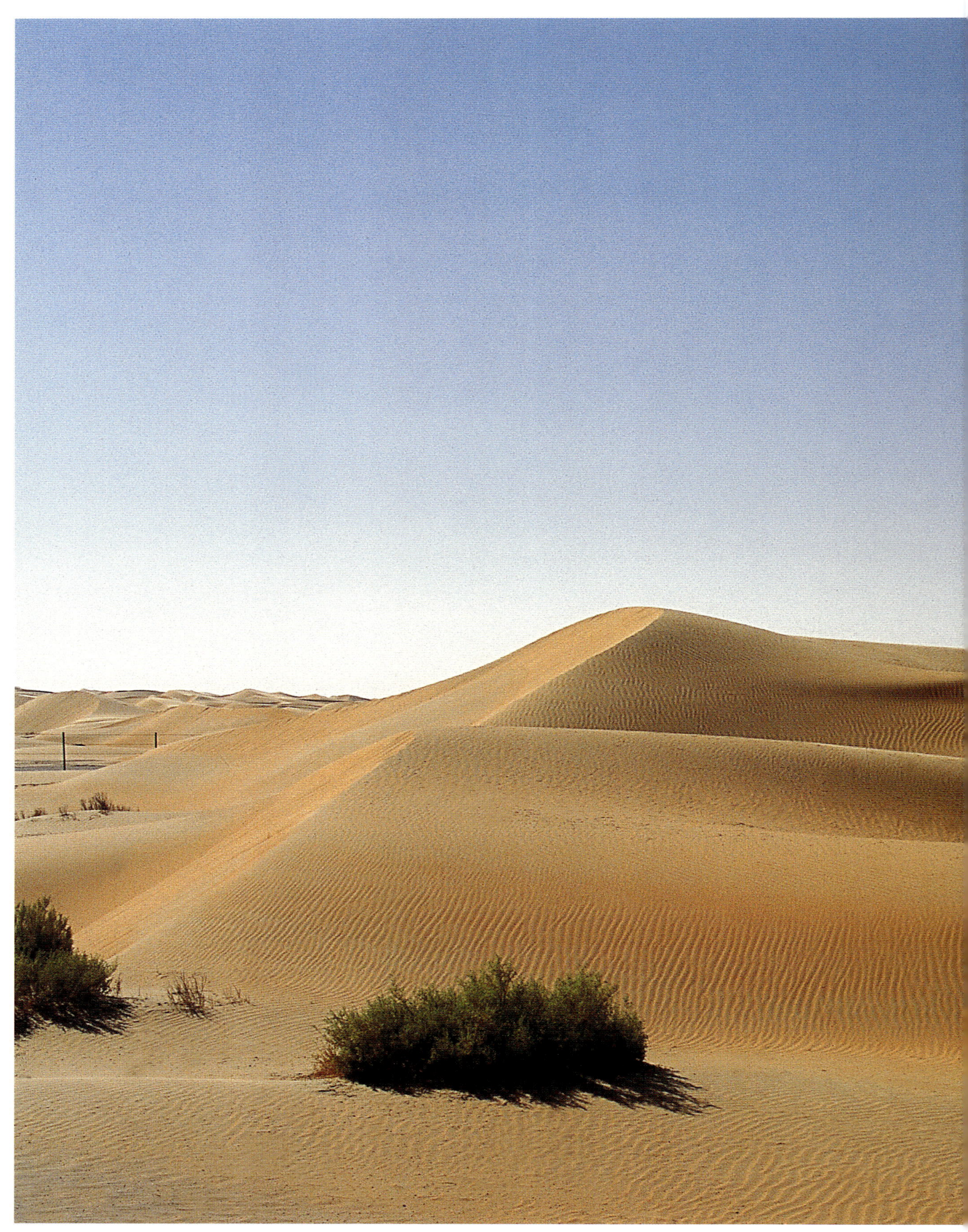

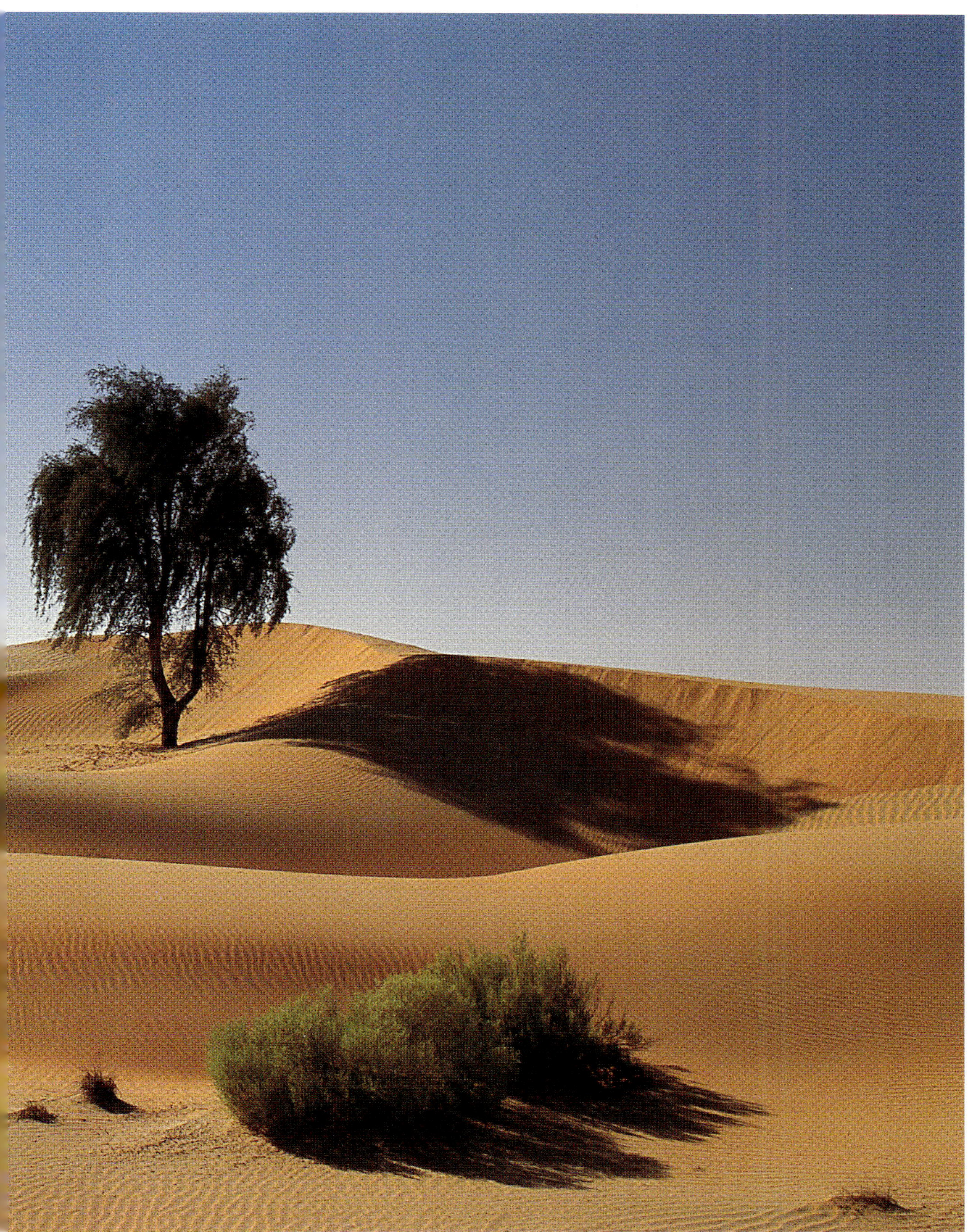

وَتَبْقَى الجِبَالُ بَعْدَنَا والمَصَانِعُ   بَلِينَا وَمَا تَبْلَى النُّجُومُ الطَّوَالِعُ

لَبِيد بِنْ رَبِيعَة العَامِرِي

We mortals wither and perish, but the stars that rise on high do not,
and the hills and the water-towers remain after we have gone.

Labid hin Rabiyya'a al-Amiri

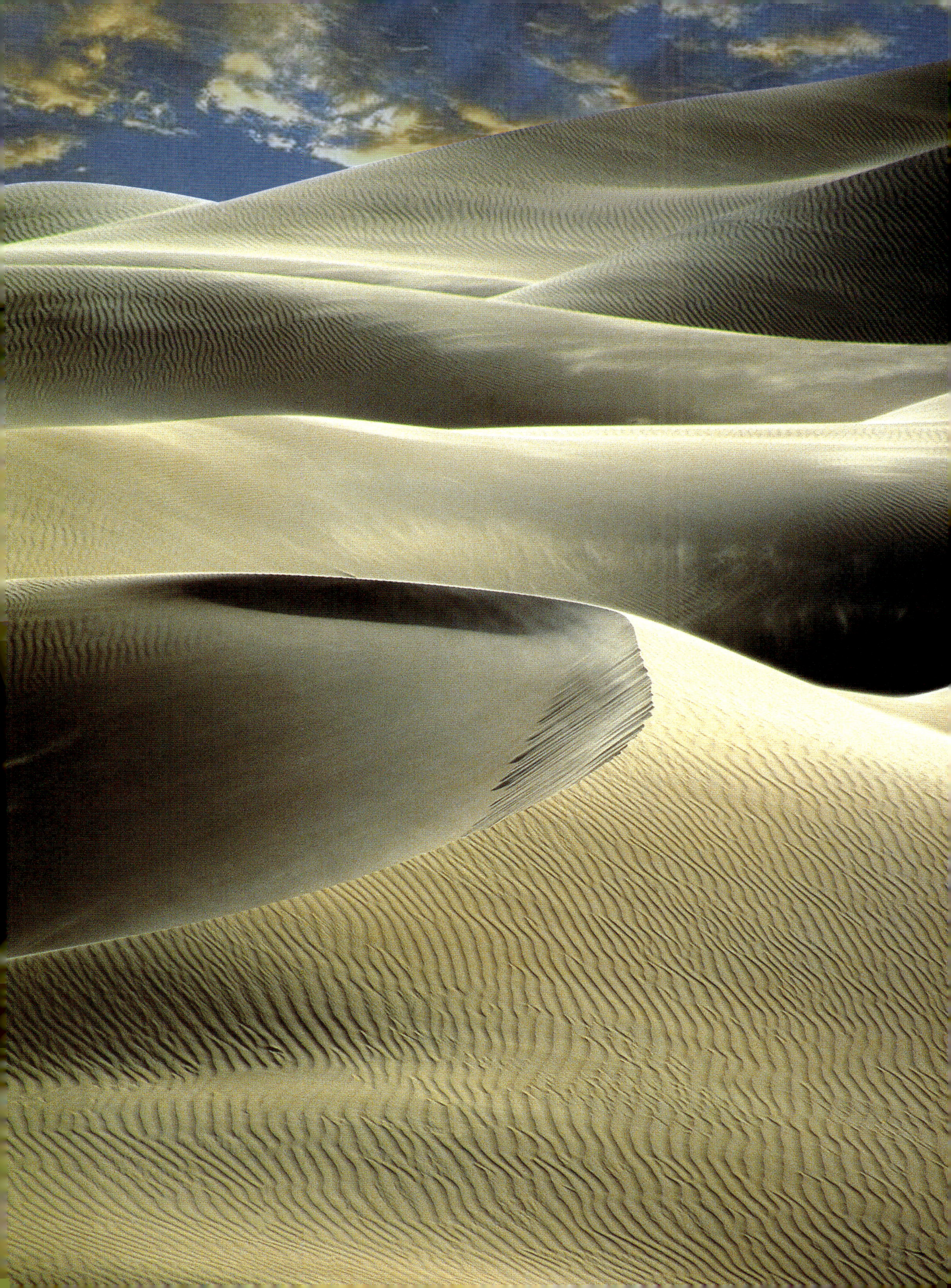

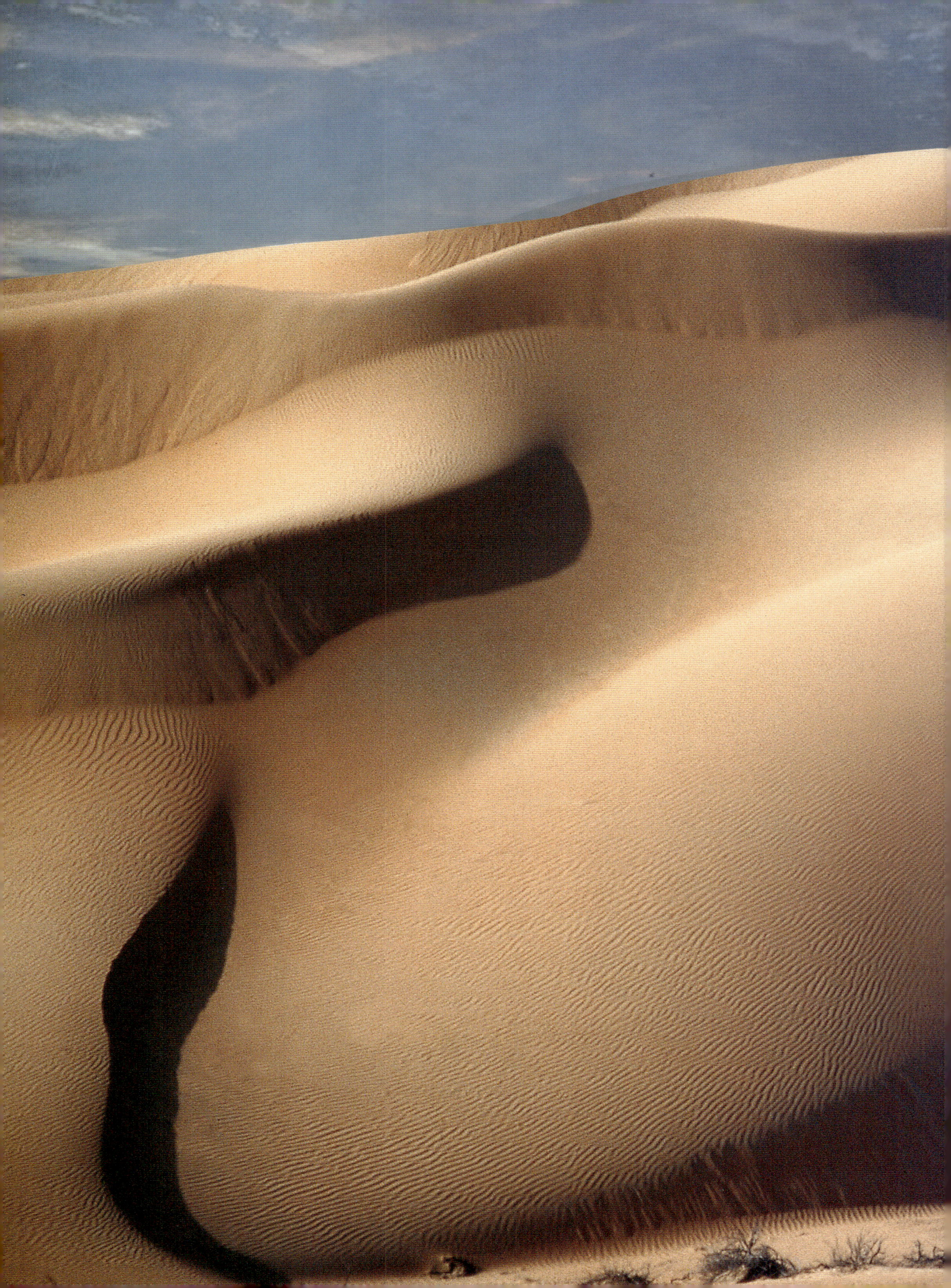

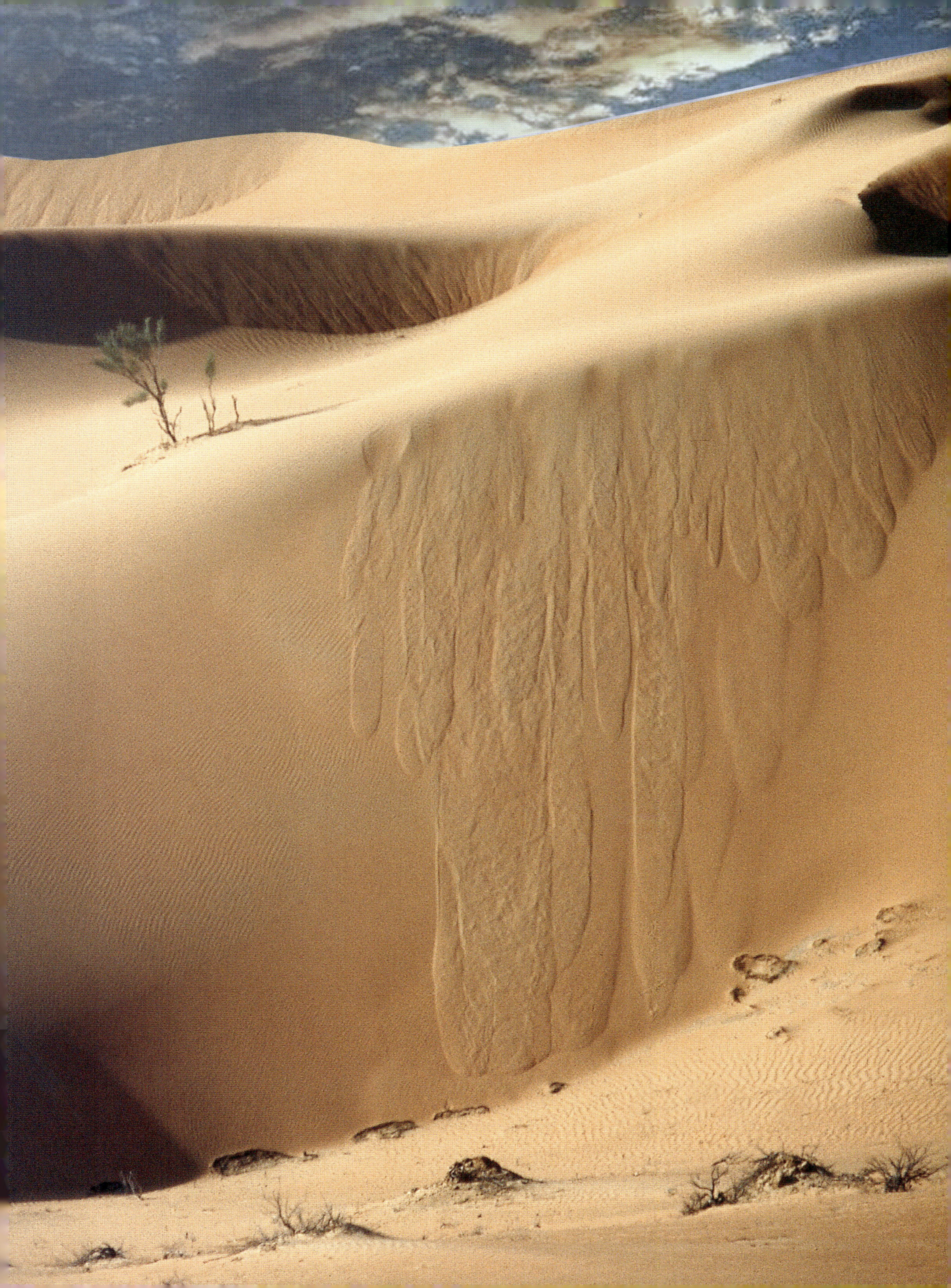

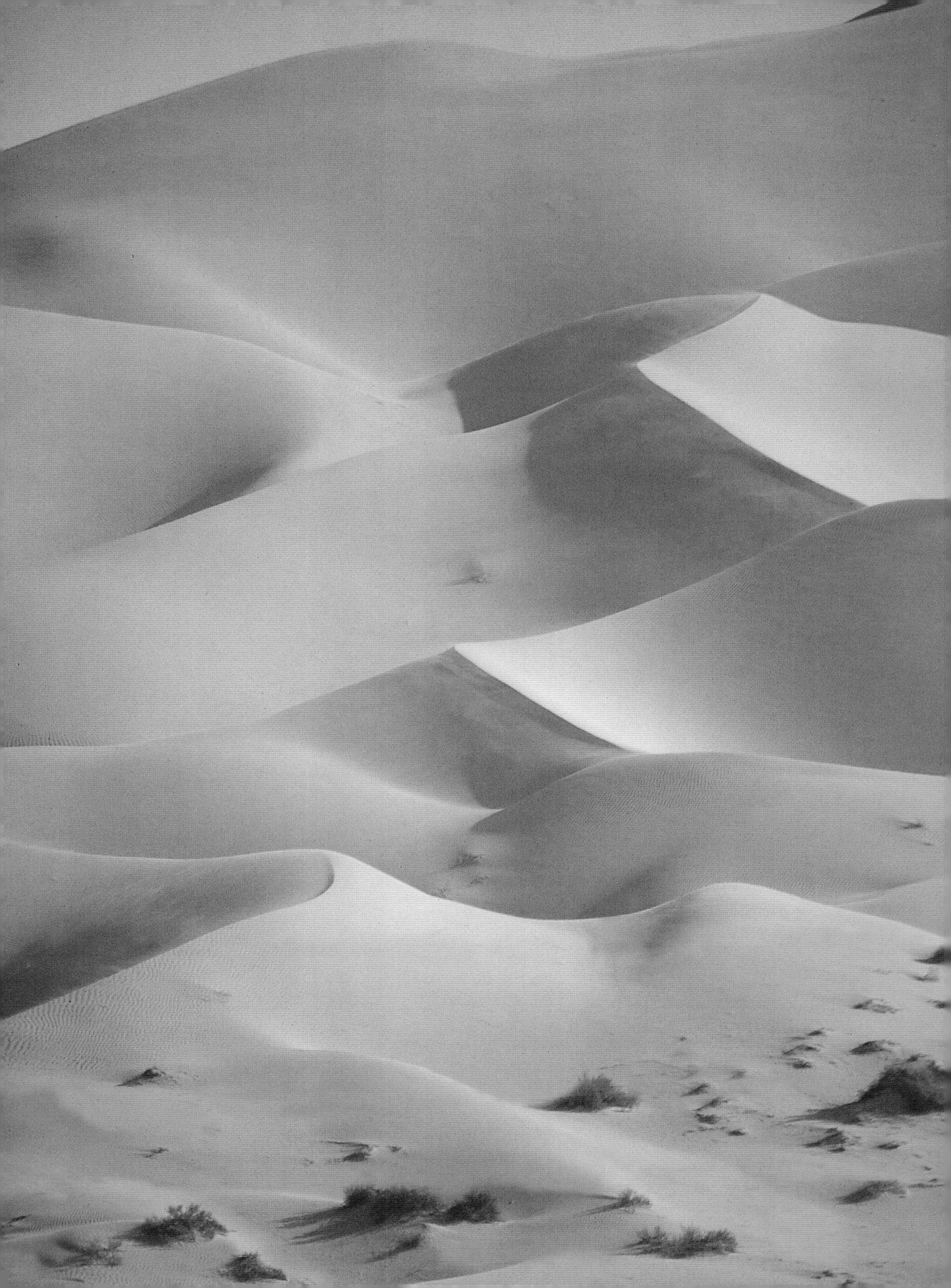

وَيَوْمٍ مِنَ الشِّعْرَى يَذُوبُ لُعَابُهُ   أَفَاعِيهِ فِي رَمْضَائِهِ تَتَمَلْمَلُ

نَصَبْتُ لَهُ وَجْهِي وَلَا كِنَّ دُونَهُ   وَلَا سِتْرَ إِلَّا الأَتْحَمِيُّ الْمُرَعْبَلُ

الشَّنْفَرَى الأَزْدِي

Many a dog-day, when the mirage melts away
and the vipers slither over the sun-baked ground,

Have I turned my unprotected face towards the heat of the sun,
with only my tattered cloak to cover me.

Al-Shanfara al-Azdi

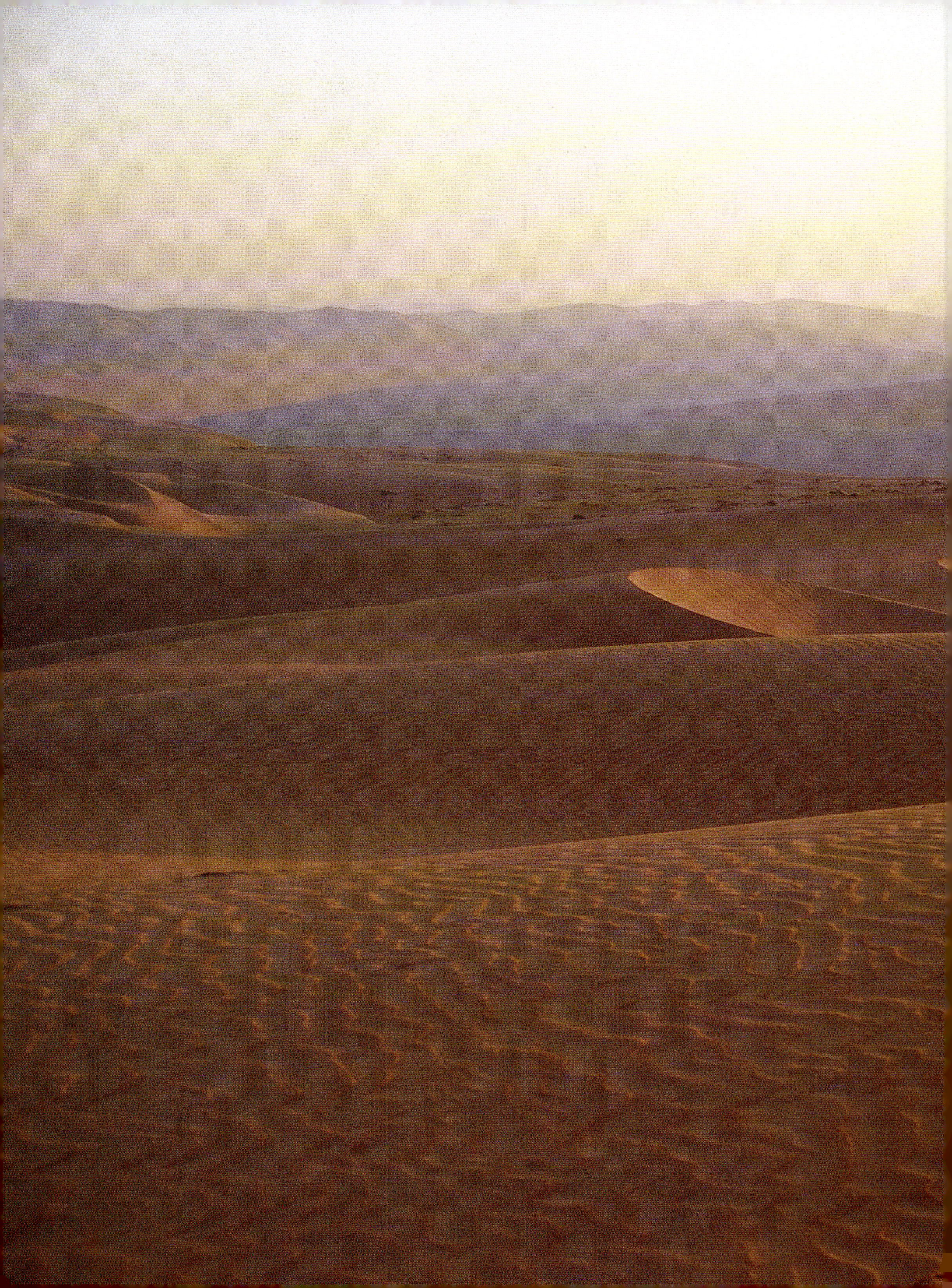

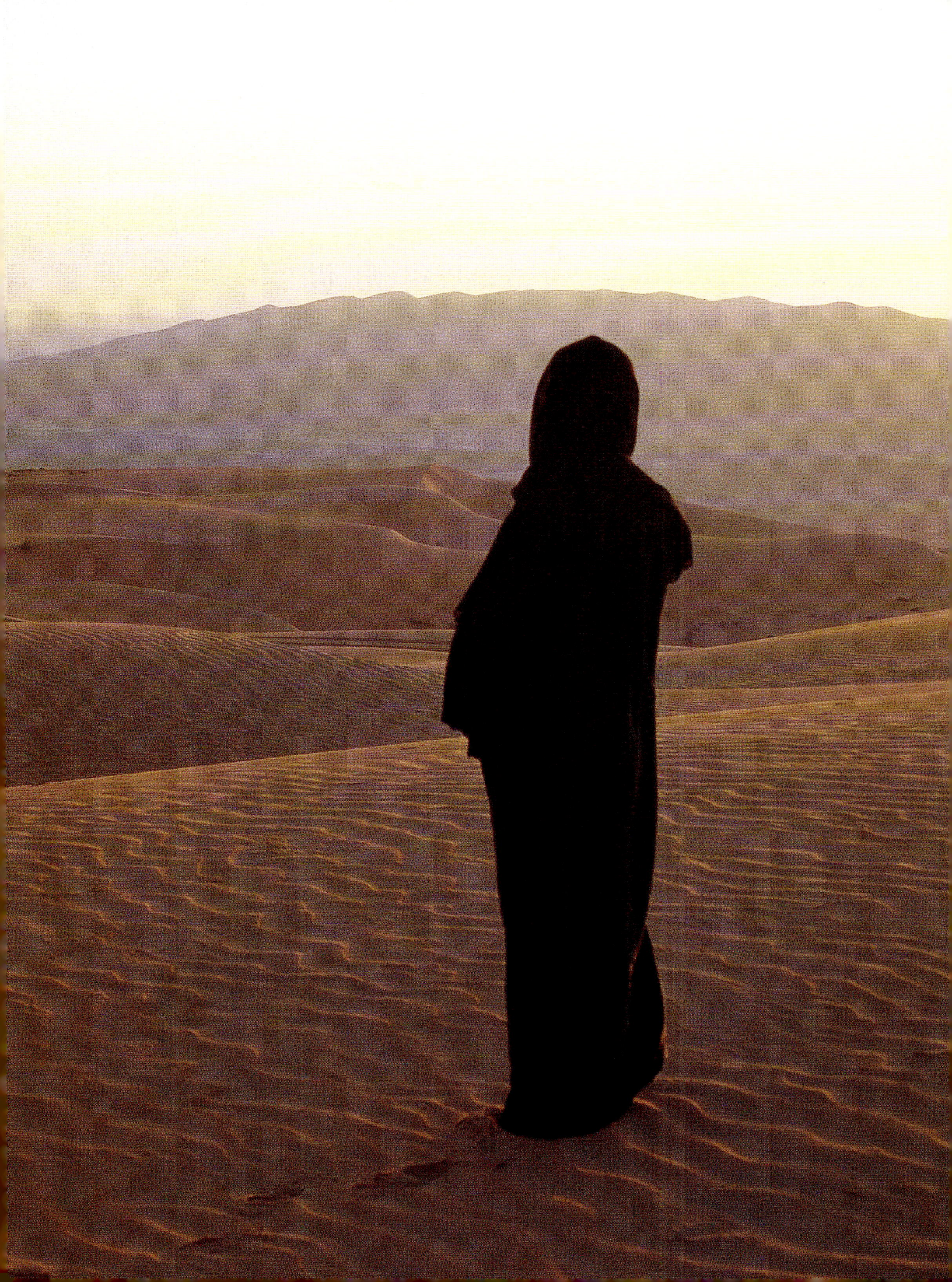

يا عِيدُ مَا لَكَ مِن شَوقٍ وإيراقِ   وَمَرَّ طَيفٍ عَلَى الأَهوَالِ طَرّاقِ

تَأَبَّطَ شَرًّا

Oh frequent memory, what yearning and sleeplessness you bring
with the ghostly image of my beloved
that comes by night, despite the terrors of the way!

Ta'abbata Sharra

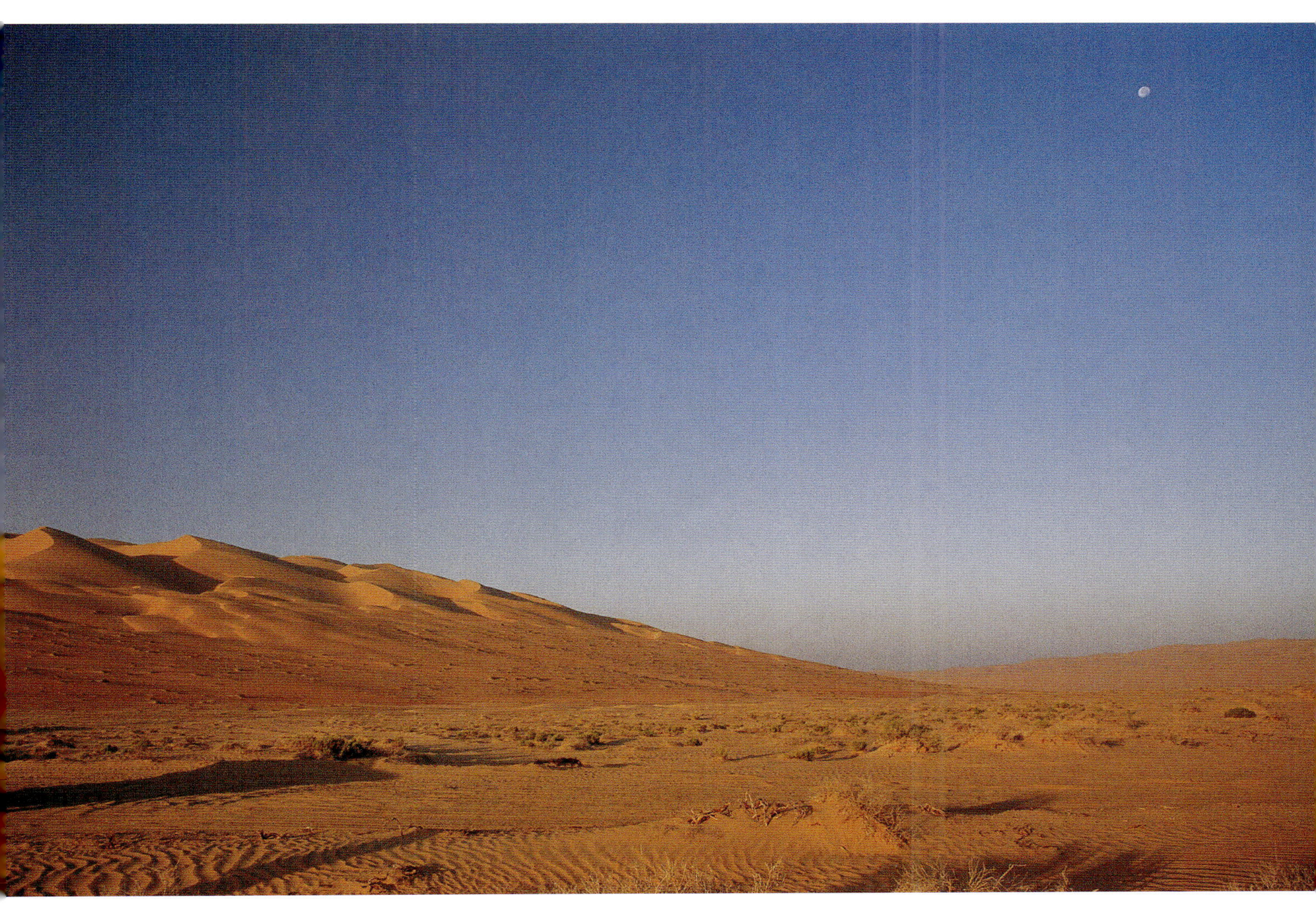

وَنَحْنُ أُنَاسٌ لَا حِجَازَ بِأَرْضِنَا   مَعَ الغَيْثِ مَا نَلْقِي وَمَنْ غَالِبُ

تَرَى رَائِدَاتِ الخَيْلِ حَوْلَ بُيُوتِنَا   كَمِعْزَى الحِجَازِ أَعْجَزَتْهَا الزَّرَائِبُ

الأَخْنَس بِنْ شِهَاب التَغْلِبِي

We are a people with no boundaries to our land.
We are to be found with the rain; and we are a people who are victorious.

You can see our horses grazing freely around our tents. They are as numerous
as the goats of the Hijaz and our enclosures cannot hold them.

Al-Akhnas bin Shihab Al-Taghlibi

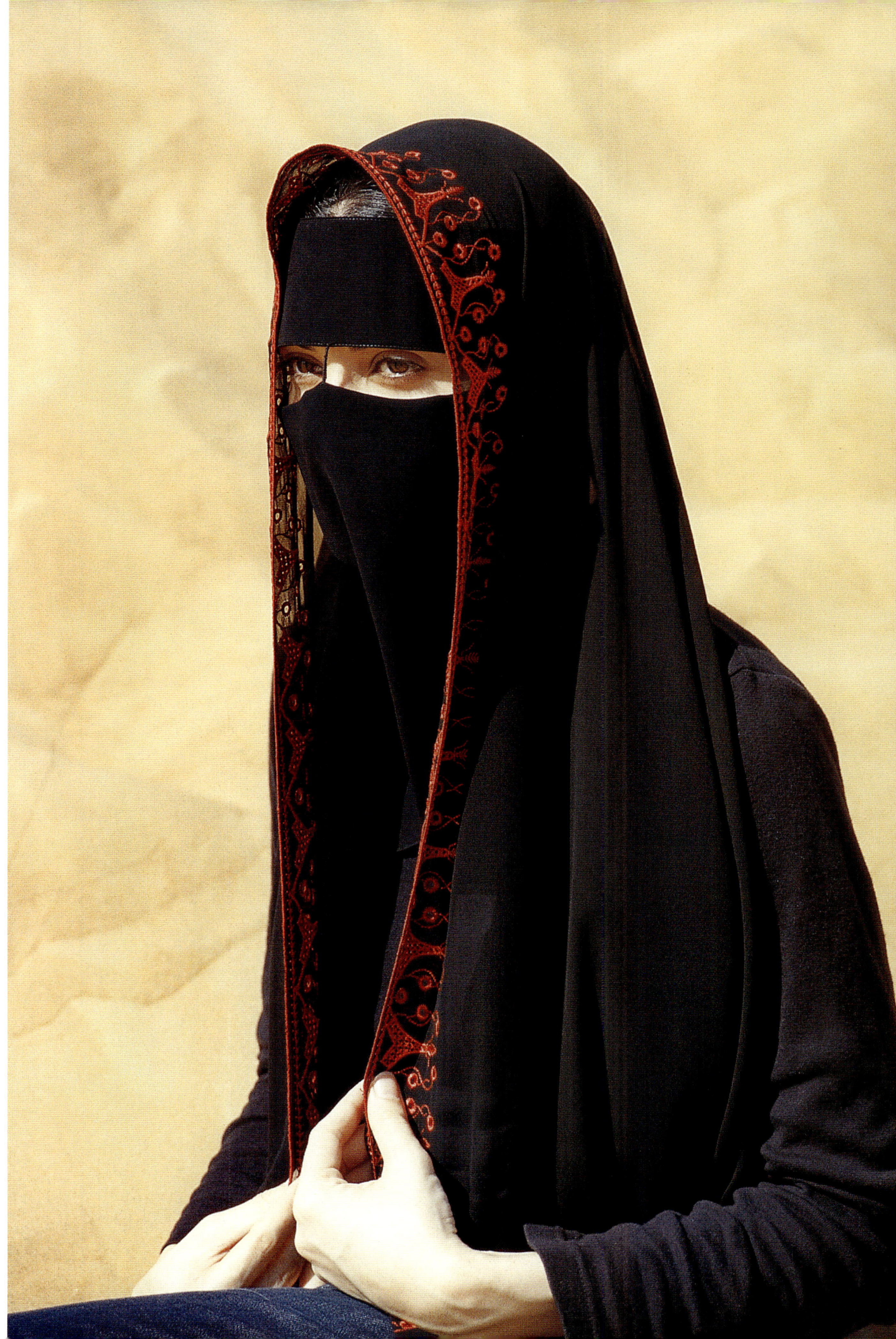

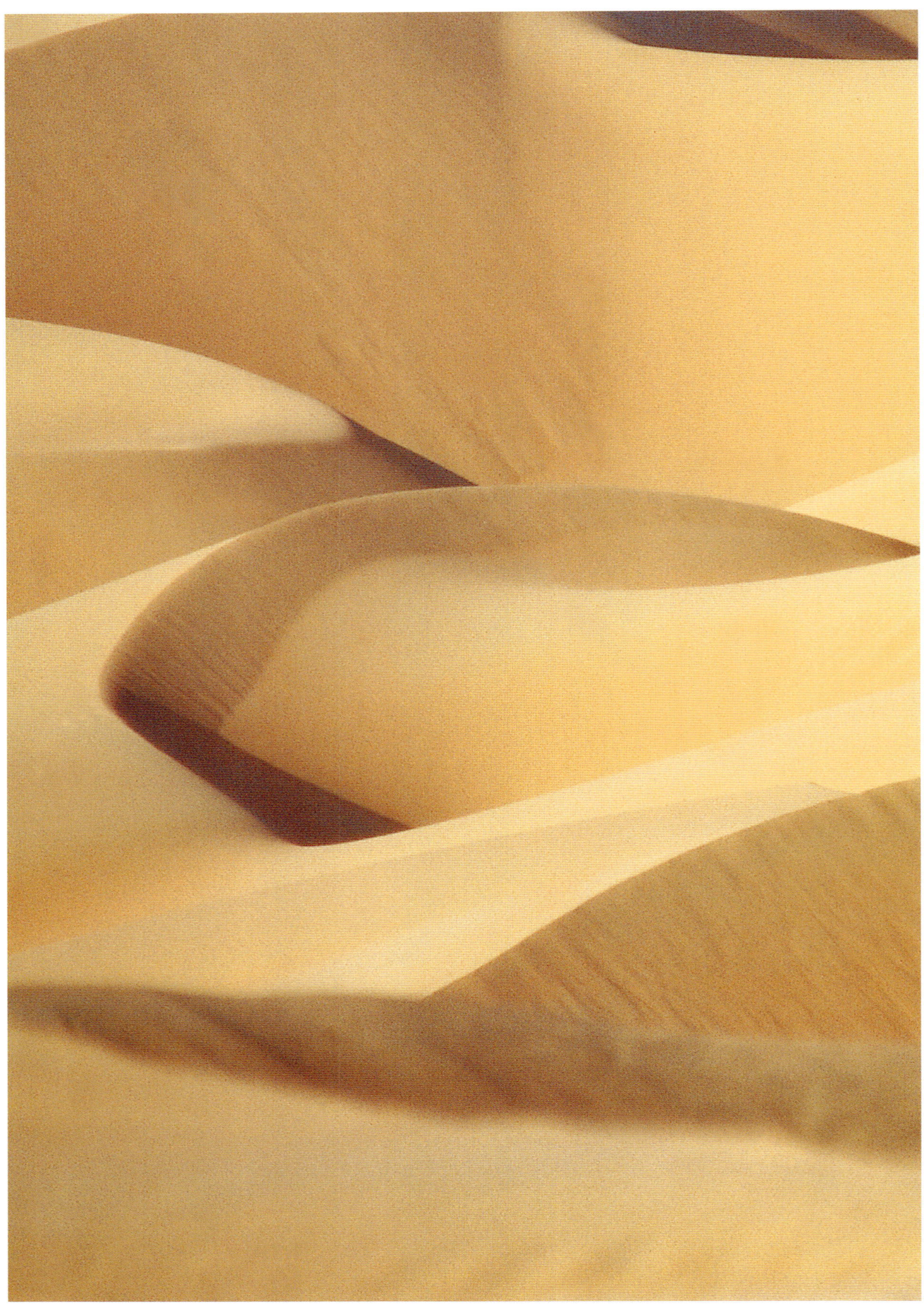